The Reflective Principal

Leading the School Development Process

The Reflective Principal

Leading the School Development Process

David Stewart
Tom Prebble
Peter Duncan

Richard C. Owen Publishers, Inc.
Katonah, New York

© 1997 by Richard C. Owen Publishers, Inc.

A first edition of this book entitled *The Reflective Principal: School Development within a Learning Community* by David Stewart and Tom Prebble was published in New Zealand and Australia in 1993 by ERDC Press, Massey University, Palmerston North, New Zealand. First edition © 1993 by David Stewart, Tom Prebble, and ERDC Press.

Library of Congress Cataloging-in-Publication Data

Stewart, David (David J.)
   The reflective principal : leading the school development process
 / Dave Stewart, Tom Prebble, Peter Duncan.
      p.   cm.
   Includes bibliographical references and index.
   ISBN 1-57274-038-8
   1. School principals—United States.   2. School management and
organization—United States.   3. Educational leadership—United
States.   I. Prebble, Tom.   II. Duncan, Peter, 1937–   .
III. Title.
LB2831.92.S74   1997   97-10140
371.2'012—dc21   CIP

RICHARD C. OWEN PUBLISHERS, INC.
PO Box 585
Katonah, New York 10536

Printed in Canada

9 8 7 6 5 4 3 2 1

Table of Contents

iii

Introduction: A User's Guide to
The Reflective Principal

This book is intended to serve as a resource and guide for principals as they lead their school communities toward more reflective and collaborative approaches to their work. Our aim in writing this book is to help schools to become effective learning communities. "School Development" is the process by which members of an institution develop the capacity to reflect on the nature and purpose of their work together. It places an emphasis on gathering data about a particular issue that confronts the school, collaboratively analyzing the data, making appropriate structural changes in the way the school works, and then, with the school working better as an organization, focusing on the improvement of teaching and learning.

The fundamental purpose of a school is to foster student learning and growth. The primary responsibility of school leadership must be to establish an environment where learning and growth are actively supported, and then to make sure they are taking place. This book also serves as a guide for a school community that wants to develop a collaborative work culture and make a difference in the learning experiences of its students.

The Reflective Principal is the culmination of more than a decade of working alongside principals. Previous publications by David Stewart and Tom Prebble (Prebble and Stewart 1981, Stewart and Prebble 1985) have encouraged a generation of principals to redefine their leadership role.

"School Development" is the process by which members of an institution develop the capacity to reflect on the nature and purpose of their work together.

This book builds on these earlier publications, drawing increasingly on the training, research, and consultancy work that have engaged David Stewart and Peter Duncan in recent years.

In *The Reflective Principal* we are suggesting a developmental process in which principals can work with their teachers and school communities. The following brief overview of the structure of the book provides an introduction to this process.

School Development is an approach that has evolved from our work with principals and schools, but it has also drawn on some of the more powerful and insightful research and scholarship in the field of school management. Part I is an all-too superficial discussion of half a dozen movements in the current research and literature on educational and general management. These themes have been selected essentially because they are saying the same sorts of things that we are. In some cases they have influenced the direction we have taken in our work. More commonly we are surprised and delighted to find that people from such different research and organizational settings seem to be heading in the same direction, and we include them here in that spirit. At the end of this section we identify an organizing matrix for the book. This matrix works on two dimensions. The first dimension concerns the level of focus for the school development process and whether the attention is being directed toward individual teachers or the whole school community. The second dimension draws a distinction between two key leadership tasks of the principal: development and appraisal. The interplay of these two dimensions suggests a program of action for the school, and also a structure for this book—school development, individual development, school appraisal, and individual appraisal. This structure can be depicted in graphic terms as a simple matrix.

Part II then outlines a model and a sequence for school development. This is designed to guide a school in its efforts to become an effective and

	School	**Individual**
Development	School Development	Individual Development
Appraisal	School Appraisal	Individual Appraisal

Matrix I

reflective learning community. The sequence has four phases: understanding the organizational culture through the gathering of data about its functioning; increasing collaboration among its members; structural changes that result from collective deliberation; and improving the quality of teaching and learning.

Part III moves from a concern for school-wide development to a focus on the individual members of the school community and the strategies that might be used to encourage greater reflection on the purposes and practices of schooling by principals and teachers. There is a discussion on reflection, its value, and ways in which it can be promoted within a school community. Quality Learning Circles are suggested as an example of promoting sustained reflection on classroom practice within a school. It is also suggested that these groups could work on a sequence of themes during the course of the school year. We have labeled this process Thematic Supervision.

Part IV takes up the theme of appraisal, considering first the appraisal of the principal and second, the appraisal of teachers. In both cases we are suggesting that such appraisal be based on a new kind of job description. This is a description of the job that recognizes that the central challenge for principals and teachers is to encourage student learning. Job descriptions should focus on the principal's responsibility to foster an effective learning culture within the school, and the teachers' responsibility to ensure that learning is taking place. All the other tasks and duties that tend to crowd into job descriptions are secondary to these challenges. We are suggesting that the principal's job description should be a relatively standard document from school to school. This document should focus the principal and district superintendent squarely on the key responsibilities of developing the school as a supportive learning community and achieving the rigorous educational outcomes we should expect from such a community. We propose an approach to principal appraisal that encourages superintendents and, through them, boards of education to engage in a cyclic process of school review.

This approach should also apply to teachers' job descriptions. The similarities in the work that teachers do in their separate classrooms far outweigh any differences that can be identified. We suggest a relatively standard job description for most teachers that focuses on the central classroom teaching activities rather than listing all of the teachers' extra-classroom activities. While the job description may be a standard one throughout the school, the way each teacher interprets that job description will vary. The way teachers think about their work is pivotal to the way they act in the classroom. We propose an approach to job descriptions that will encourage a dialogue between teachers and colleagues on how they think about their work. We are suggesting that administrators monitor the performance of each teacher and the way they interpret the challenge of their job description through regular appraisal meetings. This Professional Development Consultation cycle is integral to the appraisal process.

The techniques and strategies discussed in the previous two sections are revisited in Part V to show that they can form part of a single, if loosely structured, process of School Development within the learning community. The School Development spiral is presented as a model of how a school might continue with a School Development process over a period of time. Finally, we

discuss the Transformational Leadership approach to educational management and suggest
that it offers probably the strongest and most
persuasive case for the sort of collaborative, goal-
directed management approach we are advocating in this book.

Throughout the book case studies are used to
give life to many of the concepts that are discussed. In all cases the names of schools, teachers, and administrators have been changed to
allow anonymity. The authors are indebted to all
of those who worked with them and took the time
to talk about their practice and their journeys
through the school development process.

At this point it is important to state what
this book is *not* as well. American schools are tra-
versing difficult times. There are few signs to
suggest that the future is likely to be any easier.
School principals, district administrators, and
boards of education are looking for advice and
support about managing a declining level of educational resources–financial management, building management, and the management of that
most important human capital–teachers, special-
ists, and other staff. They also seek support in
dealing with a wide range of contractual arrangements with staff and their relationship with various stakeholders and community interests with
whom they must deal. The school's commitment
to its local community is another theme whose
importance is only just beginning to be recognized. For some schools this means facing competition for students from neighboring schools, and
for others it means a serious re-examination of
the school's commitments to local partnerships
with business interests, law enforcement, and social agencies. It can also mean serious challenges
from special interest groups within the community who feel their concerns should be better
served by the school. In some districts the closer
involvement of the community in the governance
of schools has not developed harmoniously, and

*The trans-
formational
leadership
approach
offers probably
the strongest
and most
persuasive case
for the sort of
collaborative,
goal-directed
management
approach we
are advocating
in this book.*

The key responsibility of the principal should be to develop and strengthen the learning community, to develop a culture of mutual accountability and support within the school, and to work with teachers to ensure improved programs and outcomes.

mediation between the school and the key activists may be necessary before any significant progress can be made in School Development.

This book has little to say on any of these important matters of school governance, policy, and management. This is not to minimize their importance or their topicality. These issues are undoubtedly very important in the eyes of boards and principals, and fortunately this importance is reflected in the numbers of publications and training courses that have been available recently for educational leaders. We have largely omitted mention of these matters in this book for two reasons. First, and most practically, we did not set out to write a comprehensive and exhaustive handbook for principals and district administrators about the administration of schools. There are others far better qualified to write on some of these matters and fortunately they are doing so. Second, we believe that the key responsibility of the principal should be to develop and strengthen the learning community, to develop a culture of mutual accountability and support within the school, and to work with teachers to ensure improved programs and outcomes. There are others on the school leadership team who can help manage the school resources or work on a marketing plan, but if principals lose sight of their primary role as educational leaders no one else can effectively fill that gap. Their work is primarily about improving the quality of education for every student. The educational experiences of each student will be determined almost totally by the teacher he or she is fortunate or unfortunate enough to be assigned at the beginning of the year. No amount of brilliant financial juggling by the principal will make one bit of difference to the outcome of these educational experiences, but the principal surely will make a difference by increasing the capacity of every teacher to improve teaching and learning.

Part I

An Introduction to School Development

Part I

An Introduction to School Development

Changing the way something is done with any group of people, whether school, business, or even family, involves much more than simply deciding to do things differently. Every group is made up of individuals, and these individuals bring to a group their own background experiences, beliefs, and understandings of the world around them. For any organization to change the way it does things, each member must understand and accept the reason for and the nature of the change. School development is certainly no exception.

Part I discusses some thoughts on the evolution of modern schooling in general and the role of the principal in particular. It also contains an overview of those aspects of research in education and management that impinge on school development and leadership. In part, this research has influenced the authors' own work in the field of school development and, in part, it supported the authors' independent research and experience.

As we approach the twenty-first century, the rate of social change increases. What was once taken for granted is now in question as these social pressures, economics, and technology impose new demands on our everyday lives. The changes in education are no exception, and as demands on schools shift, the role of the principal has altered to meet the new needs. In terms of an historic overview of schooling, the principal is no longer "high priest" or community leader, a factory manager, or a program director. Looking toward the future, the principal of a school is going to have to be both a learner and a leader and will have to contend with the fact that the very nature of what constitutes the school experience will be continually modified.

A great deal of research into the nature of systemic change has occurred in the 1980s and 1990s. Interestingly, many of these different schools of thought have similarities with overlapping imperatives for initiating change. Common themes have emerged. There is an increased understanding of the impact of individual belief systems on group dynamics and a corresponding call for increased communication and collaboration within organizations such as schools. Issues such as the existing culture, the amount of power and control perceived as available to different members of an organization, and methods for accepting diversity as a group strength are now of great interest to leaders in business, church groups, and service agencies.

Changing a school's culture is no different. Principals leading a change in school focus will grapple with these same issues and challenges. The process of leading change is often chaotic and fraught with challenges. From the perspective that school development is both possible and rewarding, and from their own work in schools, the authors suggest a framework to help principals guide the change process within their own schools.

As tools for understanding, organizing, and facilitiating change in a school, Matrix I and the four phases of School Development introduced in Part II look deceptively simple. The dimensions of *individual, school, development*, and *appraisal*, or a sequence of activities labeled "Phases 1, 2, 3, and 4" could be perceived as forming a tidy game board with a box marked "start." However, the reality is that balancing these processes is a great challenge and requires a skillful principal who is willing to be a reflective learner while also being a leader. In this and subsequent parts of this book, the authors offer principals a means to leading their faculties through a process of school development where a school becomes more sharply focused on teaching and learning.

Chapter 1

School Development:
The Evolution of an Idea

Recently, Thomas Sergiovanni has been called to task by one or two critics for altering his position on a number of key theoretical issues in educational leadership. Sergiovanni has been one of the leading researchers and writers in the field of educational management for over two decades, and his publishing career traverses the human resources movement, the "social sciences" approach and systems theory, the critical theory movement, the phenomenological stance, the focus on organizational culture, and most recently the interest in transformational leadership, to list just a few of the highlights of that era. The changes of interpretation and focus in the field of educational administration have been so great that some analysts speak of a paradigm shift. Sergiovanni has stayed at the forefront of this rapid evolution of perspectives. What have remained constant in his publications are his focus on the principal as an educational leader and his conviction that effective school leaders must work with their teachers rather than through them.

Educational administration must operate at the intersection of politics, sociology, psychology, and economics, and in a turbulent arena. In such a complex environment it is unlikely that any for-

Educational administration must operate at the intersection of politics, sociology, psychology, and economics, and in a turbulent arena.

7

mulation will be the complete answer to any set of problems, or that it will remain the answer for many years. Ideas and interpretations that seemed helpful and useful ten years ago have given way to fresh interpretations and new advice. Sergiovanni has shifted his perspective to accommodate new ways of analyzing the educational enterprise and its management and continued to trial new ideas and practices. Over the course of his career he has increasingly recognized that educational administration can never be an exact, objective science, and that thinking and writing about management, like its practice, must be a constant process of creating and recreating our knowledge and understanding of what we are about.

Like Sergiovanni—and for similar reasons—we authors have changed our stance on a number of issues over the years and developed new solutions that may have sometimes displaced rather than simply supplemented previous advice. But also like Sergiovanni, we maintain that our core values and focus remain unchanged.

We have long argued that the most effective locus for training or development in school management is the school itself, and that unless the whole school is involved in this process, the outcomes are likely to be limited, disappointing, and short-lived.

Some years ago Tom Prebble and David Stewart (Prebble and Stewart 1981) began a series of school-based training and development projects, attempting to involve the whole school staff and to ground the training in the problems and challenges of each school rather than on any imposed outside solution. To this end, we arrived at a four-phase model of School Development that seemed to assist schools to pace their progress in this process of school-based, collaborative organizational development.

Continuing our consultancy work with schools in the early 1980s, we found that this problem-centered orientation to school development seemed to demand a level of commitment and energy that many schools could not muster. The proposed problem-solving process required faculties to be able to work collaboratively to identify and then solve problems, something that generally lay outside the school's organizational culture and experience. We came to realize that schools needed to develop a culture of collaboration, *then* a commitment to work together to improve the effectiveness of the school, before the faculty could expect to have much success with this problem-centered approach.

Increasingly our emphasis (Stewart and Prebble 1985) shifted from helping schools to identify and solve organizational problems to developing a collaborative culture that would be able to undertake such a problem-solving program. The schools were encouraged to gather data on their current situation before launching anything new, and found that many school faculties needed practice in working collaboratively before they could be expected to embark on major new initiatives. We urged them to consolidate and evaluate their innovations carefully before proceeding too fast toward further changes. This suggested a more generic sequence of activities for schools as they went about the process of school development (Stewart and Prebble 1985).

Experience has shown that some of the ideas and techniques we advanced in our previous publications work better than others, and some emphases are more appropriate than others. Like Sergiovanni we came to place increasing importance on the establishment of a collaborative and supportive learning climate or culture within the school, and on the principal's contribution to that process.

A radical shift in the administration of education in New Zealand in the late 1980s gave every school full responsibilities for site-based management. At no time in that country had

Many school faculties needed practice in working collaboratively before they could be expected to embark on major new initiatives.

there been a greater need for schools to work together at the school site in support of teaching and learning. Since 1991, David Stewart has worked with hundreds of New Zealand principals and teachers as they have struggled to come to terms with their site-based management role. In the United States, Peter Duncan has been fortunate to study, observe, and work with administrators who, like their colleagues in countries throughout the world, try to make sense of new responsibilities. Basing part of his work on the experience of his author colleagues, Peter Duncan has worked with principals in states across the country, finding that the assumptions underlying the process of school development have equal validity in schools in New York City, Texas, Michigan, Arizona, Colorado, or Vermont and New Hampshire.

This combined experience has convinced us that "instructional leadership" and "supervision" are critically important and universal elements of effective school management. But we are less convinced that a problem-centered cycle of supervisory visits by the principal or other administrator is the most appropriate vehicle for exercising this leadership. We have used as an example of one leadership approach the idea of Quality Learning Circles that was developed over many years by David Stewart. In this approach, a heterogeneous group of colleagues reflect on their own professional practice through sharing each others' experiences. Rather than base their observations and reflections on a collection of reported problems or challenges, we are suggesting an annual cycle of themes to give structure and direction to supervisory and developmental activities throughout the school.

More than ever, principals and teachers are being challenged to demonstrate the effectiveness of their efforts. Policy makers are committed to developing and implementing systems for teacher and principal appraisals as a means toward this end. Experience in the United States, as well as observation of recent attempts in other countries, would suggest that a system of externally defined and imposed appraisal will not achieve its stated aims. Instead of encouraging excellence, creativity, and variety, it is likely to encourage careful adherence to minimal standards and conformity to the measuring instrument. Externally imposed appraisal systems will also discourage the development of collaborative work cultures within schools as teachers strive to protect any narrow advantage they may enjoy over colleagues.

We believe that an enlightened school developmental process that recognizes the importance of a collaborative learning culture is able to meet both sets of expectations. That is, it can deliver on district and state commitments for rigorous appraisal as well as help to develop a climate in which both teachers and students can achieve at the highest levels.

It has always been difficult to decide what schools should be doing, difficult to be sure that what is going on in classrooms is addressing these purposes, and often equally difficult to identify and measure the outcomes of that schooling.

The Challenge of the Principalship in Today's Schools

The school principalship has always been a demanding, stressful position. There has seldom been much unanimity over the goals and objectives of schooling, either in the community or within the teaching profession, and yet the principal has been expected to coordinate and lead the efforts of a group of colleagues in pursuit of a set of coherent and acceptable goals. The process of teaching has proved difficult to define and measure, and harder still to modify and improve, and yet the principal has always been held responsible to a greater or lesser degree for what goes on inside classrooms. Teachers have generated a set of professional values placing great stress on individual autonomy and yet expect the principal to facilitate their efforts. It has always been difficult to decide what schools should be doing, difficult to be sure that what is going on in classrooms is addressing these purposes, and often equally difficult to identify and measure the outcomes of that schooling.

None of this is new, and any worthwhile analysis of the principalship has had to take into account the ambiguities and uncertainties intrinsic to the schooling process. Models of management drawn from the fields of business and the military have had to be modified to recognize the distinctive organizational and cultural features of schools and schooling and its leadership.

This book is about leadership–school leadership. At no time in public schooling has there been a more urgent need for skillful administrators to become more skillful leaders. At no time has the task been more challenging. Nearly every group of professionals serving the public in occupations such as health care, law, social services, and education, to note only a few, is under intense community scrutiny. With one of the brightest spotlights on schools, it is hard to contemplate anyone wishing to take on one of the toughest jobs of all, that of a school principal. The job can be at once demanding, frustrating, and lonely. It can also be intensely satisfying for those with a clear vision and a commitment to achieving it. A principal is in a position of the highest trust and has a task with the noblest of intentions, but the job is too often surrounded by conflict, bitterness, and community strife that blunts a school's real purpose and saps energy from those who work in it. Yet, despite the potential tribulations, a school principal can embody the best of a community's spirit and be a power for community growth and development through what a school does for its students. That is why there are still educators who willingly seek the job.

Many issues impinge on the way principals see the task of school leadership. There are a few we can explore that have helped frame their work in American elementary and middle schools. The issues touched upon are not definitive, but are some of those currently being discussed in schools and their communities across the country. These issues include the impact of change and uncertainty on the school curriculum; the legacies left by past assumptions about schooling and how it was practiced; whether schools work best within a culture of competition; restructuring and the appraisal of principals and teachers; and two recurring themes in this book—developing a collaborative culture and using reflective practice as the developmental tool.

Change and Uncertainty

Students who graduate from high school in the first years of the twenty-first century would have entered kindergarten or first grade at the end of the 1980s. Consider the changes that occurred in the first few years of their schooling:

- the world's geopolitical balance altered so dramatically that there were profound changes in how each country viewed the rest of the world;
- scientific advances in genetics were so rapid that they outstripped clear understandings of their social implications;
- changes in information technology reshaped personal communications and the potential for our relationships with each other;
- welfare support that provided an alternative to employment as a source of family income began to evaporate;
- major corporate restructuring made career paths less certain and the possibility of unemployment for those who had never considered it a reality.

Many state and district curriculum frameworks suggest schools should be about "life-long learning" and "learning how to learn."

Changes of this order demonstrate the problematic nature of designing a school curriculum with a sufficient range of knowledge and skills to cover everything that one might need to know in an uncertain future. Indeed, many state and district curriculum frameworks suggest schools should be about "life-long learning" and "learning how to learn." This emphasis suggests that knowledge of facts and a narrow list of skills that are such a major part of school learning today are less important than developing a broad range of learning strategies for finding and using knowledge and skills in daily living.

New knowledge is being discovered all the time, placing a question mark over much of what we have taken for granted. The so-called "laws" of the physical sciences are a case in point. Theories about the chaotic and complex nature of the physical world have offered new windows into scientific study. Many argue that schools would do better to develop a curriculum that emphasizes essential, broad skills for life-long learning such as problem-solving skills, informational skills, a range of communication skills, and the like. Principals and teachers support the idea that schools are about life-long learning, but the concept inevitably raises a dilemma. On the one hand, they want to provide for a curriculum that meets the needs of all students preparing for an uncertain future, and on the other, there is a strong attraction for many communities to retain the traditional character of "their" school's curriculum. Parents see school as the one social institution that offers stability in the same rapidly changing world that makes a traditional school curriculum seem so increasingly irrelevant. They can see the school as a bastion of traditional values and a basic curriculum that would protect their offspring from the excesses of amorality and joblessness. This nostalgic view of schooling meets a need for many parents to settle for a concept of schooling that is both simple and certain.

It is simple in the sense that the traditional school fulfilled the task that the community assigned to it. It is certain in the sense that success or failure could be explained by the notion that ability plus hard work led to success.

According to Elliot Eisner (1992) traditions like this have endured because schools in the United States "are robust institutions whose very robustness provides a source of social stability." Their stability is in part due to teachers teaching as they themselves were taught and the fact that most teachers work in isolation. Reflection is a difficult process to conduct alone. Insights and new understandings are gained only when reflection becomes a group collaborative process.

Legacies

In a perceptive analysis of the history of the American public school, Phillip Schlechty argues that the way leaders "conceptualize the purpose of their enterprise will, in the long run, shape the way their organizations are envisioned and structured" (1990). He suggests that public schools have passed through three phases. In each phase the principal has had a distinctly different role.

The first, or common school phase, was characterized by schools as tribal centers transmitting a common culture. The curriculum was founded on the values of an Anglo-Saxon Protestant lore of the new republic and upheld by a principal assuming the role of a high priest and community leader, embodying the community's values. Schlechty notes that there is "a residue of sentiment shaped by myth, folklore, and oral tradition," advocating a return to this conception of schooling. Its advocates see dedicated, well-educated teachers, parent support, and respected principals ensuring "all would be well in America's schoolhouses" (1990, 21).

The second of Schlechty's phases is the factory school. This phase echoed emerging trends in the industrialization of America. It emphasized efficient scientific management where "differentiation, standardization, control and rationality became the operating guides" (1990, 22). With the factory model came the concept of school failure, engineered in part by the introduction of grades and the graded reader. These tools were designed to increase production efficiency by differentiating the operating tasks. The principal's role, Schlechty contends, shifted from that of high priest to a factory manager overseeing a range of functions necessary for producing measurable results. Supervision, coordination, and the management of time and resources became the essential prerequisites for successful principalship. The emphasis for teachers in the factory model was on technique, technical skill, and a search for the best methods of instruction. Teachers were given "teacher-proof" instructional materials, simplified curricula, and were subject to quality control through rigorous standardized testing. The factory model also had a derivative for the role of principal. In districts with strong central control, the principal was relegated to the role of a site supervisor and line manager, with product control under the direction of the district superintendent.

The harsher realities of urban industrialization gave rise to a third phase, in which the school assumed the function of a hospital. In this phase, Schlechty notes, the "legitimate purpose of schools [was] to redress the pain and suffering imposed on children by the urban industrial society" (1990, 25). Schools became the "great equalizer," providing for those disadvantaged by "injustice and inequality in society." Needy students not only received schooling in the accepted sense, but were offered supplementary services such as food, clothing, and shelter. This is clearly a more "client-centered" view of students than a factory "product" view. Students in the "hospital" school were dependent on expert support provided through a range of service delivery programs. Schlechty's contention is supported by the words and phrases that are now common parlance in schooling, such as *diagnosis, specialist, prescription, learning disability*, and *at risk*. These were borrowed from the health professions, perhaps as a response to the perceived lower status of teachers and principals when they were seen as factory workers and managers. The choice of client-centered language and the operational model of service delivery through programs could well be construed as an attempt to professionalize teaching. Both teachers and principals could elevate their status by aligning their service delivery roles with an already recognized professional group. Similarly, principals assumed more the role of program directors or chiefs of staff, rather than supervisors or managers.

The Future

Schlechty admits that his three phases of schooling would not stand the test of empirical scrutiny. Despite that, they provide useful pointers as to how and why the vision and structure of the American school takes its current form. The three phases also suggest the way principals' roles are shaped by how they perceive the purpose of their schools at any one time. If one was to look into the general culture of the contemporary American elementary and middle school, it is not too difficult to find elements of Schlechty's tribal, factory, and hospital schools blended into the mix, suggesting perhaps some lingering uncertainty as to the schools' current purpose. If, for example, we were to look at the current "program" basis for managing the delivery of remediation we find a case in point. A number of feder-

For a school to begin to work as a learning community principals have to redirect their thoughts and energies toward the purposes of the school—to "restructure" previous assumptions about traditional practices.

ally or state funded programs have been devised to target specific problems of underachievement. Schools have implemented these programs by withdrawing students from mainstream classrooms for the purpose of remediation with a specialist. There is the tendency in remediation programs to simplify the content of instruction and slow the pace of learning (Allington 1994). As a consequence, there comes a point at which these remedial students fall so far behind their peers that they are unable to return to the mainstream and are doomed to continual remediation. Thus, remediation programs become a self-perpetuating feature of contemporary schooling where many students, despite the emphasis on success for all students, will simply not succeed. In one sense programs like these take from the classroom teacher the opportunity to develop the capacity to deal with a wider range of learning needs. Equally, they take from the school the opportunity to develop a sense of mutual responsibility for the success of all of its students, since the structure of remediation appears to condemn many students to failure. This idea of developing a sense of mutual responsibility is a concept that we will discuss further, but it is also one that is an essential component of a school developing as a community.

The point of this remediation example is to suggest that for a school to begin to work as a learning community principals have to redirect their thoughts and energies toward the purposes of the school—to "restructure" previous assumptions about traditional practices such as remediation. There are signs in many districts that this redirection is taking hold. Perhaps schools in the United States are at the beginnings of a new phase of development, that of school as community (Sergiovanni 1996), where the accent is on all students finding success in learning. Here the role of principals becomes one of directing and facilitating learning, while at the same time demonstrating their own continuous learning. In communities where the roles of teacher and learner are interchanged and where members are interdependent, the glue that holds the school together is the universal process of learning.

The Power of Competition

Competition is one of the entrenched traditions in the culture of the American school. The key issue is whether raw competition operating at so many levels is consistent with the school's development as a learning community. It is not difficult to find competition for funding at the district level among schools when one measure of school status is the number of programs that any one school is able to offer regardless of whether or not they improve student achievement.

Competition also operates within a school among its teachers where they compete for status. In the early months of 1996, President Clinton convened an educational conference of business leaders to examine progress toward the educational goals set out in the national goals document (U.S. Government 1991). Participants agreed that the goals were becoming more elusive as time passed and that progress was not as rapid as it might be. The reasons were varied. One was offered by a local high school principal being interviewed about the implications of the conference for schools. He suggested that if only middle schools were doing their job properly, then the high schools could do their job much better. One can only imagine the response of the middle school principal looking toward the grade school. And what about the grade school teachers? The fourth-grade teacher turns to the third-grade teacher, suggesting that if she only had students entering her room who had all reached their previous grade level expectations, she too could do her job. Then the third-grade teacher turns to grade two, grade two to grade one, grade one to kindergarten, and the exasperated kindergarten teacher to her colleague teaching pre-kindergarten. If only the students entering kindergarten could play more happily together in the sand box, listen more intently to what they were told, and be more ready to learn, she too could do a better job in kindergarten. The pre-kindergarten teacher turns toward the parents, and the parents to their child. If the student is not progressing well at school, whose fault is it? Since there is no one else to blame, could it possibly fall on the student? Is it the student's fault that schools are not doing as well as the goals document suggests they might?

The problem with beginning a cycle of blame is that there is no logical end to it. Each level of the system is competing with the others to avoid the responsibility of being held accountable for its shortcomings, so the blame could finally rest with the most vulnerable, the very students for whom the system exists. Even the elaborate systems of diagnosis, labeling, and treatment programs that attempt to cope with failure can ultimately exonerate the system by declaring that the student's problem simply failed to respond because the student lacked ability or did not work hard enough in school.

Another example of competition in schools concerns the competition for ideas. The debate over the teaching of reading in the elementary school has become so intense in many communities that reference is often made to the "reading wars." The protagonists divide between two camps—those who favor an approach to reading instruction called whole language, and those who favor a phonics approach. This book is no place to add to the debate, other than to note that there are many faculties also divided over the issue. These faculties are divided to such an extent that teaching approaches are no longer discussed either in the faculty room or in staff meetings. Teachers go about their business behind the closed doors of their classrooms without reference to one another and usually without interference from the administration. Indeed, it is not unusual for principals to proudly declare their support for an "eclectic" approach to instruction in their schools. Debate is avoided by a tacit understanding that the reading wars can never be won and that further conflict is best avoided by accommodating the diversity of approaches in an acceptable way. At the same time, such avoidance is neither healthy for the purpose of community building nor conducive to personal or professional development by the faculty. Both are essential for school development.

There is one more example of competition that is becoming increasingly more openly encouraged. This is the competition between neighborhood schools for students. By opening places in schools on a competitive basis, whether they be magnet schools, neighborhood schools, or more recently, charter schools, the proponents argue that parents would want their students to go to the better schools. The argument goes that parents who vote "with their children's feet" send an important message to the poorer performing schools about having to lift their performance or continue to lose students. Again, this is not a place to enter this debate, but the consequences of choice as a performance motivator can have a profound effect on both schools and neighborhoods. The most telling is that parents do not really get an equal choice, since in open competition once the places in the most popular school or program are filled, there is no longer an equal choice for the remaining parents. In the end, however the choice system is worked out, there will be some parents who get no choice. Also, there will be some schools whose principals and faculties know they are regarded as failing. The issue is not so much knowing that, but how a

Teachers go about their business behind the closed doors of their classrooms without reference to one another and usually without interference from the administration.

"failing" principal can change both the perception and the reality. Beginning a process of building community would be an essential first step.

Restructuring and Appraisal Systems

Faced with considerable challenges to educational effectiveness, state and district policy makers and administrators have advocated a process of "restructuring" in their search for a solution. Restructuring is a broad and ill-defined term. It is often assumed to mean that greater educational effectiveness will be achieved by altering the organizational structures through which schooling is provided, either at the school or at the system level. "Site-based management" is one example. Granting site-based responsibilities seems to be based on the optimistic assumption that through a simple process of devolving management and professional responsibility to the site, the performance of the school will improve. This assumption fails to recognize that the primary functions of school–teaching and learning–are carried out in individual classrooms and not in the principal's office.

Restructuring has to begin with an assumption that if there is any chance of sustainable change in schools it will begin in the classrooms of teachers who are able and willing to make changes, not with policy makers trying to juggle the structural components of the system to force changes. There is little evidence to suggest that forcing structural shifts on principals and teachers, such as new funding arrangements or school choice, has ever worked in the past to increase achievement, and little reason, therefore, to suggest that it will work in the future. Neither do structural changes, like a move to site-based funding, guarantee wise decisions, just that decisions will be made differently. They certainly do not promise miracles for a failing school.

Appropriate changes to the structure of schools or systems are more likely to come as a result of changes in teachers' understandings about more effective approaches to teaching and learning. A simple example is the so-called "long block" in middle schools. Teachers who are used to 50-minute periods do not respond well to being informed that their teaching period is to double in time. However, when they have developed new understandings about effective teaching and learning, and further developed classroom practices that support students having a longer exposure to appropriate learning experiences, the long block begins to make sense as a structural change. The structural change *follows* the new understandings. Improving school practices means continually examining the assumptions that underlie existing practices.

Policy makers have not ignored the importance of changes to classroom practice in their reform initiatives. Another system-wide answer to the challenge of improving school performance has been to hold teachers more directly accountable for the outcomes of their teaching. Increasingly, the community expects teachers and principals to be accountable for their performance, and districts are being required to devise systems to reinforce this accountability. Teacher appraisal systems based on relatively objective measures of performance are intended to be the vehicle for these judgments about performance standards.

Nonetheless, attempts to measure teacher performance as an indicator of student learning are unlikely to achieve their designers' objectives of improving the effectiveness of classroom performance. It is quite possible to devise systems of teacher appraisal that will enable schools to maintain minimal thresholds of performance. We know from experience in a number of countries that teacher inspection and grading systems reinforce minimal performance and encourage conformity of teaching style. A system of school-

Attempts like this to improve educational effectiveness are based on a management model that is inappropriate to educational settings.

based teacher appraisal implemented by the principal and superintendent may enable them to reach some crude judgments about the relative effectiveness of each teacher. These judgments may then enable another series of judgments to be made about appropriate levels of reward. These systems alone are unlikely to do anything to improve the level of student learning.

Attempts like this to improve educational effectiveness are based on a management model that is inappropriate to educational settings, and may even be inappropriate in some business organizations. These approaches are probably not effective because they make a number of assumptions about schools and schooling that simply are not valid. Inevitably such approaches assume that:

- written statements of educational goals and objectives are reasonably straightforward, unproblematic, and noncontroversial, and that they provide a firm platform for all planning, action, and evaluation within the school. Instead, of course, goal statements tend to be broadly written and imprecise, and are capable of varied interpretation to the point of mutual contradiction. Given the pluralist nature of our society and its values this is inevitable;
- the interpretation of goal statements into educational programs is equally straightforward. This assumption too is demonstrably false. School policies endorsing both harsh punishment regimes and *laissez-faire* discipline can each claim to be serving the objective of inculcating a sense of responsibility;
- the link between programs and outcomes can and should be directly causal, and that the effectiveness of any educational initiative can be assessed in quantitative and standardized terms. This is skirting a millennial debate in the educational field, but there are any number of problems with this assumption. The

more complex the behavior or understanding that is being sought, the more difficult it is to demonstrate that the teaching act was responsible for the behavioral outcome. While it is theoretically possible to discount the background experience of learners, this is not easily achieved and, unless one assumes a standard level of application and ability from students, it is hardly fair to expect standard outcomes from similar teaching acts. Also, it is well known that the pursuit of standardized, objective outcome measures will encourage teachers to "teach to the test" rather than taking a broader approach, and so on;

- added effort by teachers will produce improved learning outcomes, and that feedback, advice, and selective rewards for teachers through a system of objective appraisal will produce that extra and redirected effort. In reality, unsolicited advice given under conditions of professional threat is unlikely to be internalized and acted upon by anyone;

- teaching must always be a solitary endeavor where the efforts of one teacher have little influence or relevance for other colleagues, and where competition for superior learning outcomes is the best form of motivation for teachers. Instead, the great challenge for tomorrow's schools should be to create supportive learning communities where teachers are encouraged to use each other's experiences and beliefs as a mirror to reflect on their own.

The objective of the policy makers is a laudable one: to demand greater effectiveness from the school system, and to hold principals and teachers responsible for achieving that effectiveness. Most principals appreciate that an externally imposed system of teacher appraisal falls well short of that target. We shall explore the first five schools of research in the following chapter, leaving the transformational approach until Part V.

Chapter 2

A Confluence of Ideas

In the past two decades there have been some significant leaps in understanding what constitutes effective schooling and how the principal's role and leadership practices contribute to that effectiveness. This chapter identifies several of the more important approaches and shows how their findings and recommendations are remarkably consistent with one another. These approaches form a backdrop to our own approach to School Development set out in the chapters following. Our approach to School Development is a highly practical and applied one. Indeed, School Development is the reflective principal at work, and as a process it is part of a strong, international movement in the theory and research literature. Its recent pedigree is worth exploration. The schools of thought that seem to be arriving at the same message for school leadership are:

- the movement to reinterpret supervision as a school-based collegial process;
- the research on effective schools;
- the "cultural" approach to the study of educational administration;
- the quality assurance and Total Quality Management traditions, both within education and more broadly;
- an earlier line of research that explored the ex-

pansion of influence within collaborative institutions;

- the "transformational" school of educational leadership, which is discussed in the last chapter.

Collegial Supervision

The pressure being brought to bear on principals and teachers to become more directly and visibly accountable for the quality of their work is not a phenomenon unique to the United States. School systems throughout the Western world have recognized that teacher competence is one of the most important determinants of educational quality. Over the past decade there has been a strong movement to establish systems designed to assess and enhance that competence by direct observation and supervision of teaching practice.

This movement has taken two directions. Probably the dominant movement in North America, and increasingly in Europe, Australia, and New Zealand, has been an effort to identify the skills and behaviors that are consistent with effective teaching, and then set up systems of supervision to reinforce these skills within the classroom. This orientation has been described as "bureaucratic" by some observers (Darling-Hammond and Sclan 1992) in that it holds that the skills of effective teaching can be specified for a system as a whole and made mandatory for all teachers. This position is based on the following five fundamental beliefs about teaching and learning:

- learning is the process of accumulating bits of information and isolated skills;
- the teacher's primary responsibility is to transfer this knowledge directly to students;
- changing student behavior is the teacher's primary goal;

- the processes of teaching and learning focus primarily on the interactions between the teacher and individual students;
- thinking and learning skills are viewed as transferable across all content areas (Nolan and Francis 1992, 45).

These beliefs are reinforced by some of the research into effective teaching that seem to support a particular style of teaching. This style exhibits a highly organized syllabus that sequences material appropriately; clear and unambiguous explanation of concepts; the use of examples, illustrations, and modeling of desired skills to reinforce students' understanding; checking of students' comprehension of the material; structured practice skills to reinforce long-term memory; and regular testing of skills acquisition.

Confidence in this position has been strong. As noted with reference to the "factory" conception of schooling in the previous chapter, policy makers have engaged in a search for the "teacher-proof" curriculum, and for instructional systems that can be made mandatory within school systems. Once a curriculum and associated instructional systems become mandatory it then becomes possible to measure teachers' compliance with the mandated teaching style through objective measures of desired behaviors.

Since the 1980s there has been a strong movement toward system-wide programs for teacher supervision and assessment. This movement has had its spearhead in the United States, where teachers are required to undergo an approved system of evaluation based on state-developed performance observational instruments. A leading prototype for such appraisal systems has been the Florida Performance Measurement System. This instrument requires observers to tally teacher behavior in two columns, one for "effective" behaviors, and the other for "ineffective" behaviors, the judgment between the two

Policy makers have engaged in a search for the "teacher-proof" curriculum, and for instructional systems that can be made mandatory within school systems.

The "professional" approach resists the attempts to wrest all important decisions about curriculum and instructional methodology out of the hands of the classroom teacher.

having been made by the designers of the instrument.

A full critique of this "bureaucratic" orientation lies beyond the scope of this book, but the following should indicate the main thrust of the criticism. To begin with, the critics would challenge the research basis for the effective teaching movement. Most research on learning outcomes has concentrated on the teaching of lower-order skills and knowledge rather than on higher-order conceptual and analytic skills and values acquisition. It is therefore not surprising that such research finds support for a highly structured, teacher-directed style of instruction, with lots of repetition, examples, and checking. In attempting to apply the findings of this research to all classroom teaching, policy makers are failing to recognize that learning should be more than the acquisition of a narrow range of specified skills. They are forcing teachers to "teach down" to a narrow instructional orthodoxy and severely penalizing teachers with a wider or brighter image of their profession.

There is an alternative approach to supervision that has been labeled the "professional" orientation (Darling-Hammond and Sclan 1992, 7). This approach resists the attempts to wrest all important decisions about curriculum and instructional methodology out of the hands of the classroom teacher, but more importantly it is based on a different set of assumptions and beliefs about teaching and learning:

- all learning, except for simple rote memorization, requires the learner to actively construct meaning;
- students' prior understandings of and thoughts about a topic or concept before instruction exert a tremendous influence on what they learn during instruction;
- the teacher's primary goal is to generate a

change in the learner's cognitive structure or way of viewing and organizing the world;

- because learning is a process of active construction by the learner, the teacher cannot do the work of learning;
- learning in cooperation with others is an important source of motivation, support, modeling, and coaching;
- skills learned in one subject may not be as easily transferred to other areas as previously thought (Nolan and Francis 1992, 47–48).

This model makes greater demands on teacher and learner, but it also offers greater scope for both. If learning implies the construction of new knowledge, it is not enough to expose students to the new knowledge and then coach them in its application. It is not sufficient to teach a new concept; learners must incorporate this new understanding into the way they understand the world. The same principle applies to teachers. It is not enough to expose teachers to new techniques and understandings about their craft; unless they have had the opportunity to test these practices, to reflect upon them, and perhaps modify them to suit their particular circumstances and challenges, it is unlikely they will be able to make the most effective use of the new practices.

The implications of this model for supervision are profound. It would suggest that an approach which specifies the "one best way" of teaching, and which requires teachers to exhibit an approved set of teaching behaviors, will encourage superficial compliance rather than full-blooded commitment to that new way. The professional approach to supervision would hold that teachers develop in their craft by being challenged to reflect on their assumptions about what they are doing and by critiquing those assumptions and practices in collaboration with col-

Only when teachers are exposed to other models of teaching and called upon to discuss their own assumptions and methods of teaching with colleagues are the prerequisites for genuine development of new understandings present.

leagues. Research and theory on learning and curriculum can be an important addition to that process.

This model would dispense with standardized instruments as the primary medium for teacher supervision. It would also jettison the claim that the expert supervisor is in the best position to identify shortcomings and suggest improvements in teaching practice. The focus of supervision should be upon teacher improvement and development rather than on formal appraisal. Schools need systems of supervision that challenge teachers to reflect on what they are doing, why they are doing it, how successful they are, whether it is worth doing, and whether there might not be better alternatives. This sort of process is unlikely to thrive within a hierarchical supervisory relationship where the supervisor is also being required to make summative judgments about the teacher affecting job security and conditions of employment.

Collaboration is an important element of this new approach to supervision. Teaching is an isolating occupation and prone to the self-reinforcement of current practice and thought. Only when teachers are exposed to other models of teaching and called upon to discuss their own assumptions and methods of teaching with colleagues are the prerequisites for genuine development of new understandings present. Judith Little (1983) maintains that by collaborating with colleagues teachers gain instructional depth, range, and collegiality. As teachers commit themselves to a team approach to supervision, a culture of professional interdependence develops, encouraging the group to attempt new approaches to their work (Grimmett, Rostad, and Ford 1992).

The raw material for much of this discussion and reflection must be data collected from classrooms. But it must be a much richer, broader vein of data than that sought by standardized observational instruments. If teachers are seeking to help their students to construct new knowledge, it will not be sufficient merely to gather data on the teachers' compliance with an approved battery of teaching techniques. They will also need to gather data on how individual students are responding to the program and how they are constructing new knowledge.

The other important dimension of this collaborative, professional kind of supervision is an emphasis on *reflective transformation of practice*. Reflective practice is a concept that extends beyond the theme of supervision and is discussed in a later section. At this point it will suffice to note that proponents of this professional approach to supervision believe that it is one of the most powerful ways in which teachers develop their classroom practice. Working with a colleague, a teacher attempts to identify or "frame" a problem in the classroom situation, and then both draw on their joint repertoire of experience and knowledge to explore explanations and possible solutions for the situation (Schön 1987). This is a focus on the teaching and learning tapestry rather than a predefined set of outcomes. A deceptively simple concept; we shall return to it in more detail throughout this book.

The Effective Schools Movement

In 1966 James Coleman published his influential study on the relationship between socioeconomic background and student achievement, *Equality of Educational Opportunity*. This study seemed to show that the impact of socioeconomic background was far more influential than the school system in contributing to differences in educational achievement by American children. In 1972 the Rand Corporation published an important study on behalf of the President's Commission on School Finance. The authors were looking for the determinants of educational effectiveness but had to come to the dismal conclusion that "research has not identified a variant of the existing system that is consistently related to students' educational outcomes" (Averch et al. 1972, 37).

These conclusions seriously weakened the faith of policy makers, educators, and the community alike in the ability of the schools to make a difference to the life chances of the young. Large-scale correlational studies in other countries reached similar conclusions and posed a standing indictment of public educational systems, showing them to be ineffective.

This conclusion tended to prevail until a landmark publication by Michael Rutter et al. in 1979. In *Fifteen Thousand Hours: Secondary Schools and Their Effects on Children*, Rutter adopted a different research methodology to the traditional approach of correlating individual student outcomes with other variables. His team identified a small number of schools within the inner-London region whose student intake was drawn from lower socioeconomic strata, but which seemed to be doing significantly better than the average against a number of straightforward measures of student achievement. He was then able to show that these schools had a number of features in common, setting them apart from the bulk of average to underachieving schools.

A rash of studies followed publication of the characteristics of these "effective" schools, and from their results educators started to promote a profile to which other schools could aspire. Ronald Edmonds (1972) was in the vanguard of this movement, and he claimed that effective schools are characterized by the following:

- strong leadership by the school principal, especially in the instructional program;
- an atmosphere that is safe and orderly;

- school-wide agreement on goals that emphasize basic skills;
- shared teacher expectations for high levels of achievement by all students;
- continuous assessment of student performance that is related to instructional objectives.

A study by Wilbur Brookover and Larry Lezotte (1979) confirmed that effective schools tended to exhibit strong consensus among teachers on goals, a clear sense of an institutional mission, and a focus on student achievement. These early studies, and many that were to follow, found that the contribution of the principal was crucial in creating school effectiveness. Kenneth Leithwood and D.J. Montgomery (1982) surveyed the research literature about effective and ineffective principal behaviors and came to the conclusion that the contribution of the principal to classroom achievement had been grossly underestimated.

In summary, effective principals are able to define priorities focused on the central mission of the school and gain support from all stakeholders. Their actions impinge on almost all aspects of the classroom and school that are likely to influence achievement of these priorities. They intervene directly and constantly to ensure that priorities are achieved (Leithwood and Montgomery 1982, 325).

These studies prompted a series of school improvement projects, mostly in the United States, which aimed to incorporate these research findings in school-level practice. Schools were encouraged to adopt the five qualities of effectiveness that Edmonds had identified. There was a renewed emphasis on student achievement, time-on-task, and applying the principles of effective learning that Madeleine Hunter had helped clarify. And a great many schools, particularly those in lower socioeconomic areas, reported significant

Wilbur Brookover and Larry Lezotte (1979) confirmed that effective schools tended to exhibit strong consensus among teachers on goals, a clear sense of an institutional mission, and a focus on student achievement.

It is always dangerous to leap from description to prescription, and a strategy aimed at inculcating the characteristics of so-called effective schools may not have the intended consequences at all.

and even dramatic improvements in student achievement in core skill areas. In their efforts to spread these practices and qualities still faster, district boards and state governments were attracted to the notion of an approved mode of teaching and an objective system for assessing teachers' progress toward this mode. And here the effective schools movement joined forces with the bureaucratic school of supervision that was introduced in the previous section.

There has been some criticism of the research that underlies the effective schools movement, and of some of the prescriptive inferences that have been drawn from that research. It has been argued, for instance, that most of the schools sampled were in low socioeconomic areas where school failure was the norm rather than the exception. "Effective" schools in that milieu may have very different characteristics from effective schools drawn from more typical schools. Most of the effectiveness research used standard measures of basic skills of numeracy and literacy to identify their samples of effective schools, rather than attempting to test for higher-order skills and knowledge. This may mean that the methods used to help a school in a low socioeconomic area to ensure an improvement in the achievement of its students in core skills will be different from the methods required to assist a typical middle-class school in becoming truly outstanding.

The school effectiveness research has also been criticized for being at best case studies, and at worst anecdotal descriptions. There is little longitudinal data to show how the effective schools got that way or how (or if) they are able to sustain that status. It is always dangerous to leap from description to prescription, and a strategy aimed at inculcating the characteristics of so-called effective schools may not have the intended consequences at all.

Notwithstanding the criticisms, the school

effectiveness movement has been a powerful one. David Clark, L.S. Lotto, and Terry Astuto (1984) reviewed the converging fields of the research on effective schools and the more prescriptive pursuit of school improvement. They agreed with D. MacKenzie (1983) and S.C. Purkey and M.S. Smith (1982) that effective schools were "vital, changing, interacting groups of people not to be represented by ingredients but, rather, by a 'syndrome' or 'culture' of mutually reinforcing expectations and activities" (Clark, Lotto, and Astuto 1984, 49). Having made that important point they somewhat apologetically advance their own list of qualities of effective schools drawn from the research literature. They published their article hard on the heels of the Thomas Peters and Robert Waterman best seller, *In Search of Excellence: Lessons from America's Best-Run Companies* (1982), and the Purkey and Smith list of qualities bears more than a passing resemblance to the Peters and Waterman list:

- *commitment*—the school community has a strongly articulated sense of mission which permeates the life and activity of the whole institution;
- *expectations*—teachers have high expectations of themselves and their students. They expect success and work positively to achieve it;
- *action*—there is a bias for action, for solving problems, and for seizing opportunities;
- *leadership*—the principal takes a prominent role in establishing the institutional mission and leading from the front. But there are also opportunities for other teachers to exercise leadership in a climate which encourages people to work together toward shared goals;
- *focus*—there is a strong collective focus on the task at hand, and most commonly this relates to student achievement and classroom activities;
- *climate*—the school is a pleasant and support-

ive environment to live and work in, for both students and teachers. At a minimum, it is an orderly and safe place;

- *slack*—there are sufficient faculty resources to enable teachers to spend some time away from classroom teaching on a regular basis. This time is essential to encourage faculty and program development activities by groups of teachers (Purkey and Smith 1982).

This list of qualities is clearly broader than that identified by Edmonds, but one that follows in the same tradition. Patricia Duttweiler attempted a review of more recent literature (1991) and found a still richer picture. Like the previous studies she found that effective schools concentrate on student learning, have clear organizational missions and goals that are shared by all, and hold high expectations for all members. But she also found that effective schools:

- are student-centered, treating students as full members of a learning community rather than as vessels to be filled with knowledge;
- offer academically rich programs that address higher- as well as lower-order skills;
- have a positive learning climate that is open, friendly, and culturally inviting, as well as being goal- and achievement-directed;
- foster collegial interaction among teachers;
- have extensive faculty development in which the teacher evaluation system is used to improve teachers' skills and the emphasis is on sharing knowledge and techniques;
- practice shared leadership, working through a team approach to problem solving and program management;
- foster creative problem solving, turning problems into shared challenges;
- involve parents and the community.

This final picture of the effective schools is certainly a richer one than the lean model proposed by Edmonds ten years earlier. It is also a more complex model, and one that does not lend itself to simplistic management and pedagogic solutions imposed from beyond the school. If schools are to develop the qualities of shared leadership, collegial interaction, positive learning climate, and creative problem solving identified by Duttweiler, they are going to need to learn how to do this for themselves.

The Cultural Perspective of School Management

As Phillip Schlechty noted in his conception of the development of the American school, during the first few decades of this century, writers on work organizations found the machine to be a powerful conceptual model for their analyses. A machine is a carefully designed set of individual components brought together to achieve a particular task. In the application of this model to organizations, theorists focused on systems of organization and supervision and measures of efficiency. In the 1940s and 1950s the attention of organization theorists shifted to the human members of organizations rather than the structures within which they were expected to work. This perspective was reflected in the human relations and human resources management theories, and continues to inform management thinking to this day. The 1960s' systems theory seemed to provide another powerful perspective on organizations and the way they operate. Systems theory encouraged attention to the relationships among the elements of an organization and to the way an organization survives within its larger environment. Another influential perspec-

If schools are to develop the qualities of shared leadership, collegial interaction, positive learning climate, and creative problem solving identified by Duttweiler, they are going to need to learn how to do this for themselves.

*All organiza-
tions have some
sort of cul-
ture–"the way
we do things
around
here"–which
shows in the
values and
beliefs to which
members gener-
ally subscribe.*

tive, and one with close links to systems theory, has been the political view of organizations. Here the emphasis is on policy development and the interplay of different interests in arriving at organizational policy. Conflict, bargaining, and goal-setting become subjects of interest to management theorists.

Each successive theoretical perspective has served to focus attention on a fresh aspect of organizational life. Existing perspectives have not been replaced, but they have become less dominant. Since the 1980s the cultural view of organizations has offered a refreshingly different view of the way organizations operate. According to this perspective, organizations are artificial entities–complex expressions of the intentions and beliefs of their members. It is necessary to understand their intentions as well as observing their behavior. According to this perspective, it has not been possible to arrive at universal laws of organizational behavior. Behavior can only be understood within its context of cultural significance and individual and group intention.

All organizations have some sort of culture–"the way we do things around here"–which shows in the values and beliefs to which members generally subscribe. Most organizations will have more than one identifiable culture, and these will tend to correspond to the social or work groupings to be found within the organization. Members of the organization will interpret their experience in terms of the cultural values they hold most strongly, and they will be most committed to activities that are consistent with those values.

This view of organizations has considerable implications for leadership. It will not be enough to design a perfect system and then require members to comply with it, as the efficiency model would suggest. It will also not be sufficient to seek the compliance of members by meeting their individual needs for security, self-actualization, and the like as the human relations/resources theorists might suggest. And an understanding of the complex interplay of elements within and without the organization, as the systems/political theorists would suggest, is unlikely to offer any practical course of action to the leader. The cultural perspective, on the other hand, proposes a vital role for leadership in defining, shaping, and promoting the core culture of the organization.

This relatively new management stance is reminiscent of the work of Philip Selznick who, some years ago, proposed that the core tasks of leadership were to define the mission of the institution, and then to infuse the institution with that mission and purpose (Selznick 1957). This very simple but powerful formula has become almost an obsession in corporate management over the past decade. In the new era of accountability, managers of corporations and public sector agencies alike speak of the major shifts of culture they need to undertake to allow their organizations to reorient themselves to a new operating environment. And many companies attribute their commercial success in large part to their ability to redefine the cultures of their organizations and to win strong support for those cultures from their employees.

The cultural perspective has proved particularly powerful when applied to educational organizations. It has provided analysts such as Thomas Sergiovanni and John Corbally with a whole new focus on the school and schooling (Sergiovanni and Corbally 1984). It has also suggested a fresh approach and focus for school leadership. In the past, most attempts to alter classroom practice have focused on the individual teacher, attempting to change practice through training and classroom intervention and supervision methods. However, an understanding of the culture of the typical school suggests that many of these efforts run counter to core cultural values. Schools are characterized by norms of professional autonomy and isolation (Lortie 1975). Or,

The challenge then is to shift the culture of the school from a traditional one to one where teachers are prepared to collaborate at the level of exploring new understandings and developing new classroom practice.

as Andrew Sparkes put it more caustically, "the ambiguous celebration of isolation masquerading as autonomy" (1991, 9). These norms are "sacred," or in Eisner's term, "enduring" in most schools and not easily altered by management intervention (Corbett, Fireson, and Rossman 1987). At the same time, there is some evidence that efforts to alter classroom practice and develop teachers' skills are most successful when there is a norm of collegiality and experimentation within the school (Little 1982).

The challenge then is to shift the culture of the school from a traditional one, where most norms of professional autonomy and isolation are sacred and paramount, to one where teachers are prepared to collaborate at the level of exploring new understandings and developing new classroom practice; from a school organization where goals and mission direction are the preserve of the leader to a school community where policy becomes a statement of effective practice. There is a growing body of research and practice that has this objective as its central purpose (Grimmett, Rostad, and Ford 1991). Though, as Bruce Joyce concedes, "the culture of the school has proved to be a very tough customer indeed" (Joyce 1990, 34).

Total Quality Management

If culture was one of the important foci for management thinking during the 1980s, quality has been another. In 1980 Western audiences viewed a television documentary—"If Japan Can, Why Can't We?"—that highlighted the growing disparity between American and Japanese industrial performance. For the first time viewers were introduced to the philosophy and methods of W. Edward Deming, one of a group of American management experts who had helped transform

Japanese industrial and management practices
since World War II.

During the following decade the Quality
Management or Total Quality Management
(TQM) approach has become one of the most influential and dynamic movements in Western
management. Its influence has spread from man-
ufacturing and other profit-based industries to
the full range of governmental agencies, hospi-
tals, voluntary organizations, schools, colleges,
and universities. Its proponents claim that it can
even help to reorient home life in more productive and satisfying ways.

Deming remains the most important authority in the area, and his "fourteen points" continue
to serve as the guiding principles for most attempts at Total Quality Management (Walton
1986). Other influential writers, such as Joseph
Juran and Kaoru Ishikawa, have arrived at
slightly different formulations, but the fundamental tenets remain the same. John Jay Bonstingl, an American educator who is making an important contribution to introducing Total Quality
Management philosophy and practices to American schools, believes that these tenets can be reduced to just four (Bonstingl 1992):

1. **The organization must focus first and
   foremost on its suppliers and customers.**
   In Total Quality Management everyone is
   both a supplier and a customer. Students are
   the primary customer of the services of teachers and administrators, but they are also "supplying" their parents and the community at
   large with educational progress and growth.
   Teachers are supplying a range of services to
   students, but they are also consuming services
   provided by their colleagues, the school, and
   system administrators. Within this philosophy
   it is important to identify the nature of these
   relationships and to keep the notion of service

to the customer at the fore. Total Quality Management advocates a collaborative relationship between suppliers and customers, with the former constantly striving to improve the level of service to the latter. The relationship between administrators and teachers is also that of supplier to customer, and Total Quality Management favors a collaborative management style that strives for continual improvement and self-development rather than control and compliance.

As Kenneth Freeston puts it more succinctly, "When we acknowledge that the student is the customer, learning is the product, and teaching is the service, we put ourselves in the position of achieving legitimate school improvement" (1992, 13).

2. **Everyone in the organization must be dedicated to continuous improvement, personally and collectively.** Total Quality Management is essentially a collaborative process whereby groups within organizations examine their objectives and their work, gather data on their performance, identify ways of improving that performance, trial these alternative methods, and then gather further data on the impact of these changes. It cannot work effectively without a culture of collaboration, and without the resources and encouragement to engage in this continuous process of group work.

3. **The organization must be viewed as a system, and the work that people do within the system must be viewed as ongoing processes.** People cannot be expected to perform effectively if the organizational structures and systems within which they work are flawed. Total Quality Management encourages organizational members to identify the shortcomings in their work systems and to constantly strive to refine them.

When applied to the process of schooling, this principle would direct attention to the process and quality of teaching and learning, rather than to an exclusive concentration on learning outcomes. While improved learning outcomes may be the final goal, they can only be achieved if teachers and students have been able to develop better teaching and learning processes.

4. **The success of Total Quality Management is the responsibility of top management.** Total Quality Management is not some subtle, subversive, bottom-up process of change. It can only work if the whole organization becomes thoroughly committed to the culture and values of Total Quality Management. And this can only take place if senior management actively leads this major cultural shift, and takes every opportunity to promote these objectives and values.

In an educational context, the primary role of leadership becomes the promotion of effective learning by all students. All the other traditional roles of school management–such as teacher and resource management–become secondary to this key role. Schools embarking on Total Quality Management spend a lot of time identifying their vision and making sure that this vision is strongly endorsed within the organization and contributing community; they gather extensive data on systems, performance, and output, and constantly repeat these measurements to test their progress; they use group processes to decide on priorities for attention, to discuss the data, and to arrive at structural and system changes designed to improve performance; and they make a commitment to evaluate these developments and to integrate the more successful innovations within the culture and structure of the school.

*Control has
taken on such
negative and
value-laden
connotations
that it has
been virtually
dropped from
the vocabu-
laries of school
administrators.*

Control

The management theories the authors have been discussing are generally supportive of a collaborative style of leadership, but one which recognizes the importance of the individual as well as the importance of the group to organizational well-being. Further support comes from an unlikely quarter–from the study of organizational control and influence.

Control is a subject that has fallen from favor since the early days of scientific management. It is certainly a subject that finds little place in the contemporary literature on school management. Principals are said to "facilitate," to "enable," to "organize," to "plan," and even to "lead," but seldom if ever to "control." Control has taken on such negative and value-laden connotations that it has been virtually dropped from the vocabularies of school administrators. This is unfortunate because regardless of the misconceptions of the term or the passing fashions in management theory, control remains a pivotal function of management, and to be deprived of its use, even as a conceptual tool, severely limits and distorts our view of school administration. The study of managerial control takes us straight to the central issues of organizational management in a way that many of these more acceptable terms do not.

Organizations imply control. An organization can be thought of as a group of people drawn together to pursue some collective purpose. An organization is an ordered arrangement of human behavior. Control processes are necessary to ensure that the behavior of members conforms to this ordered arrangement. However voluntary the association, and however simple the task, there will need to be some coordination and order brought to bear on the individual efforts of members. Arthur Tannenbaum defines control as "any process in which a person, or group of persons, determines, that is, intentionally affects the behavior of another person, group or organization" (1968, 5).

Tannenbaum's definition starts to clarify the process of control, but it also reveals why control is such a controversial process. The manipulation or influence of one person's behavior by another cannot ever be considered merely a technical matter. There is an enormously important moral and ethical dimension as well. Control raises issues such as the rights of the individual over the rights of the group, the legitimacy of organizational authority, the morality of enforced compliance with organizational norms, and the right to dissent.

All principals are familiar with the autonomy/control dilemma. Time and again they are forced to strike a balance between the need to ensure compliance with organizational goals through control and the equally important need to allow their faculty the fullest possible expression of their individual, professional autonomy. These decisions are made considerably more difficult if principals believe that every delegation is made at some cost to their own authority. Such a belief is based on incorrect assumptions about the nature of organizational control and its distribution.

The "Influence Pie"

A basic assumption underlying many arguments over autonomy and control is that in any organization there is a fixed amount of control available for management to use. That is, if managers share, say, 30 percent of the control of their organizations with their workers, they will retain only 70 percent for themselves. Conversely, some human relations theorists advocate power equalization, in which a manager's fixed amount of power is distributed evenly among all the members of an organization. In terms of Tannen-baum's definition of control this assumption is demonstrably false. Control is not a fixed quantity, and management and workers are not engaged in an all-or-nothing struggle over its distribution.

The easiest way to demonstrate this is by the example of a weak, permissive manager, where there is little exercise of control in terms of attempting to influence the behavior of members toward desired ends. It is likely that the other members of the organization exercise a similarly small amount of influence over each other's behavior. In such an organization behavior tends to become increasingly idiosyncratic, coordinated working relationships break down, and people pursue their own ends. In short, the total amount of control in the organization is relatively small. If that manager is replaced by a more energetic, task-oriented person then the total amount of control being exercised in the organization will almost certainly increase quickly as the new manager starts to bring influence to bear on the behavior of other members. If that same manager then encourages members to share in important management decisions, set team goals, and supervise each other's work, the total amount of control being exercised will have risen again. At each step organizational behavior becomes more goal-directed, more ordered, and more coordinated, and more members of the organization come to acquire influence in shaping the behavior of their colleagues and themselves. In short, the *total amount* of control increases. The crucial point is that the manager need not lose personal control by encouraging other members to exercise control themselves.

Tannenbaum and his associates (Tannenbaum 1968; Tannenbaum and Cooke 1979) have completed dozens of empirical studies into the distribution and amount of control within work organizations. The evidence from these studies suggests that:

- organizations with influential rank-and-file members are likely to be more effective than those with uninfluential memberships providing that the officers are not less influential in the first than in the second group of organizations;
- organizations with powerful officers are likely to be more effective than those with less powerful officers, providing that the membership is not less influential in the first than in the second group of organizations;
- organizations with influential leaders and members are likely to be more effective than organizations with less influential members and/or leaders (Tannenbaum 1968, 309).

Paraphrasing these carefully worded if somewhat opaque statements, the authors conclude that a collaborative leadership style will only be truly effective when leaders retain a high level of control. The findings contradict the traditionalists who hold that the total amount of control in an organization is fixed. The evidence shows that strong leaders lose no control by encouraging members to collaborate in key decisions. The findings also tend to contradict those advocates of shared decision making who are opposed to any form of control by leadership. Tannenbaum has shown that a high level of member participation and control is not inconsistent with hierarchy or strong leadership control.

Another way of summarizing Tannenbaum's findings is to say that the amount of control in an organization seems to be an important predictor of member commitment and organizational effectiveness, whereas the distribution of control within an organization seems to be less important. This finding is quite consistent with the human resources school of management that advocates a more active involvement of members in the organization and a higher total amount of control than is common in most bureaucratic or-

A collaborative leadership style will only be truly effective when leaders retain a high level of control.

ganizations. A common stereotype of collaboration with shared decision making is of a loose permissive system in which members are free to pursue their own goals. In fact the opposite is the case for most supporters of shared decision making. Human resource theorists such as Rensis Likert (1967) advocate a highly coordinated "organic" type of organization in which control is exercised through a network of relationships and dependencies. According to theorists such as Likert, an organic collaborative style of management encourages a high level of commitment from members and is characterized by a high level of total organizational control. The success of collaborative approaches, Tannenbaum suggests (1968, 23), hinges not on reducing control, but on achieving a system of control that is more effective than that of other systems. Likert has coined the term "influence pie" to refer to the total amount of control being exercised within the organization. The pie may be cut and shared in many different ways, but the best way to ensure that everyone gets a bigger slice is to bake a bigger pie.

Limits of Control

In the previous section an argument for the importance of control in the leadership of educational organizations was presented. A naïve interpretation of the research on control and effectiveness might suggest that a high level of member collaboration coupled with strong leadership control is a realistic and straightforward goal for all school principals. In fact there are many difficulties and constraints associated with any attempt to increase the total amount of control or its distribution within schools. Principals need to be aware of these constraints before they attempt to alter the balance of control.

Tannenbaum is an advocate of organic, collaborative models of leadership that imply a high level of total control as well as broad distribution of that control. Organizations with high levels of control tend to have the following qualities:

- *strong internal linkages*—reporting and supervisory relationships are clearly laid down; each division of the organization is closely linked with related divisions; and the work of each member of the organization has a direct and measurable effect on other members of the organization.
- *high levels of inclusion of members*—members are able to apply most of their skills and talents to the performance of their work; they enjoy it and are committed to the goals and activities of the organization.
- *resources that can be exchanged for compliance*—such organizations are able to persuade members to comply with organizational programs and objectives through a wide range of rewards and resources. These might include: the ability to hire, fire, and promote; social approval; financial advantages; status; and access to training opportunities and needed experience.
- *low levels of confusion and conflict*—most members understand and agree with the objectives of the organization; they understand how to perform their work; there is little conflict among members; and little resistance to the initiatives of leadership (Tannenbaum 1968, 23).

Yet, we cannot take for granted that these are common features of schools. Typically, schools do not measure up well against any of these attributes:

- schools tend to be characterized by low connectedness of members and activities; the cel-

Teachers may well resist what they see as an unwelcome increase in the control of their work by other members of the faculty.

lular organization of schools contributes to "loose coupling" and minimal contact between teachers during the working day; school administrators typically exercise little influence over classroom practice;

- schools tend to display a low level of inclusion of members. The uncertainties intrinsic to the teaching act challenge the efforts of supervisors, evaluators, and trainers, and disincline teachers to practice their craft in the full glare of public attention;
- in most school systems there is a paucity of resources that can be exchanged for teacher or student compliance;
- there is a constant state of conflict in most school systems over the means and ends of the schooling process. A multiplicity of conflicting and ambiguous goals sanctions almost any activity but frequently defies any evaluation of effectiveness.

These organizational features all in varying degrees militate against the success of organic, participative models of management in schools. They suggest that increasing the size of the influence pie will not be a simple or straightforward process. Teachers may well resist what they see as an unwelcome increase in the control of their work by other members of the faculty. They may also resist more active participation in organizational decision making. This resistance need not deter a principal from attempting to influence the work of classroom teachers, or from involving these teachers in more of the organizational decision making, but it should be anticipated in the change strategies that are used.

As a school begins to take a serious look at goals and effectiveness—embarking on School Development—the manner in which control and influence is exercised within the organization becomes of central importance. The first stage is to examine and debate the levels and patterns of control that currently operate. Many schools will find that there is scope for a considerable expansion in their influence pie, but what would it mean for a school to expand the size of its influence pie until everyone had a big enough slice? In general terms it would mean that both the principal and the faculty would begin to exercise much greater control over the key achievements of the school. More particularly it would mean the following kinds of development. There is more likely to be:

- a better knowledge base within the organization; all teachers would have a good working knowledge of the major organizational and instructional systems operating within the school; organizational problems would be investigated on the basis of reliable data collected and shared by the teachers themselves;
- greater clarity in school policy and goals and explicit guidelines about the extent to which individual programs could depart from these shared goals;
- regular teacher participation in decisions concerning school goals, organizational procedures, and institutional programs; in general, teachers would be involved in all decisions in which they needed and wanted to participate; where individuals choose not to participate in the decision making they may need to agree not to obstruct group decisions;
- regular programs for the supervision of work; teachers would receive regular support from colleagues to help with the development of their understanding and classroom practice, to maintain standards, and to coordinate classroom programs;
- consistent and comprehensive evaluation of student progress and all teaching and learning programs;
- a commitment to using the resources of the school to solve individual and organizational

problems; and a prevailing norm of "your problem is our problem";

- general participation in key decisions concerning the allocation and use of instructional and financial resources, and effective control procedures to ensure compliance with these decisions;
- negotiation of the commitment from individual members of the faculty to the work of the school, coupled with a willingness to accommodate individual differences;
- a deliberate attempt to relate to the environment beyond the school in an active rather than a passive way;
- a commitment to cooperate fully with agreed policy and procedures, and in exchange for this commitment there would be a willingness to renegotiate all agreements on a regular basis.

The study of control takes us not into a technology of domination and manipulation, but toward the values and practice of collaboration and participation. It reveals that strong leadership and participative management constitute an effective and compatible combination. It also suggests an approach to management that may be particularly well-suited to managing a group of professionals.

A Confluence of Ideas

In this chapter we have discussed five contemporary movements in educational and management theory: the collegial supervision movement; the effective schools movement; the cultural perspective of school management; the Total Quality Management approach; and an approach to control that favors an expansion of influence within collaborative organizations. Each of these movements goes beyond the relative

safety of description and analysis and suggests a
line of action for the practitioner. To this extent
they are prescriptive theories, not content to analyze what is, but bold or foolhardy enough to suggest what should be.

What is particularly interesting is that in
their prescriptions these approaches have much
in common with one another. While they may differ in the sequence of development and in emphasis they can be shown to contribute to the following assumptions:

1. **Learning requires the individual to actively construct meaning and knowledge
   on the basis of reflecting upon experience.** Learning takes place when individuals
   are able to build on existing knowledge to
   make sense of new experience. It is not simply
   a matter of transferring existing knowledge
   from one person to another. Learners bring
   their own experiences and abilities to the new
   experience, and this will influence the way
   that learning takes place.

   Given such a view of learning it will not be
   possible to arrive at a universal formula for effective teaching. Each learning context and
   each group of learners will require its own
   unique teaching approach. Teachers themselves learn and develop in their craft by reflecting on what they are doing, why they are
   doing it, and the effect it is having.

2. **At an organizational level, this view of
   learning requires members of the school
   community to gather data systematically
   on the key processes they are endeavoring to develop, and to reflect collectively
   on the significance of that data.** An individual is able to make sense of the world
   through processes of introspection and personal reflection, yet may have difficulty ex-
   plaining how opinions are arrived at and deci-

The principal's main objective should be to foster a climate of active reflection and learning throughout the whole school community.

sions reached. An organization, on the other hand, must be far more systematic and explicit in its processes of collective decision making. If an organization is to "learn" in the way that has been described, it must develop ways of reflecting collectively upon its experience. This involves at least two stages. First, it must discover and share its experiences through a process of guided data gathering and research. Second, members must have the opportunity to reflect on the data they have collected and the significance and implications of those data.

3. **The primary objective for the principal is to establish a learning community.** If principals seriously believe that learning is the active construction of knowledge by individuals, then they will not be satisfied with any school goal that emphasizes mere knowledge acquisition. The principal will want to establish conditions that encourage students and teachers to challenge old conceptions and learn from new experiences. It is the process of reflection and learning that we will be focusing on, rather than merely the outcome in terms of knowledge acquired. The principal's main objective should be to foster a climate of active reflection and learning throughout the whole school community. This objective certainly extends beyond the student body. Teachers too need to be reflecting on what they are doing and the effects of their actions. Parents need to be brought into this net of learning and reflection too. They cannot rely on prepackaged or yesterday's solutions any more than students and teachers can. They need to share in the process of a developing school community gathering data about itself and reflecting upon it.

4. **The principal has a critical role in developing a core culture dedicated to learn-**

ing and ensuring that the establishment of the learning community becomes the major preoccupation for all members of the school community. As Karl Weick noted in 1976, schools are loosely coupled organizations in which actions and developments in one section of the school may have little or no impact in another, and in which leaders and managers have only indirect influence over what happens in classrooms (Weick 1976). Ten years later he refined this analysis by conceding that administrators in loosely coupled systems achieve influence by shaping the culture in which teachers work and the perceptions and values they share (Weick 1986).

In short, the principal cannot hope to control the direction of the school by directing the daily operations of classroom teachers as if they were factory process workers performing interlinked and easily monitored tasks. The best way to influence that direction is to identify, clarify, and modify the core culture of the school, perhaps in the form of a mission statement, and then to take any and every opportunity to articulate and model those beliefs, values, and shared understandings to enhance learning.

5. **The development of a culture of collaboration and mutual accountability is a necessary step on the path to the learning community.** While in theory it may be possible for teachers to improve their practice through private introspection, wide experience would suggest that this is not an especially effective method of teacher development. Teaching tends to be a solitary act, where patterns of practice are reinforced rather than challenged by frequent and unchallenged repetition. Experience from many educational and management perspectives suggests that

teachers learn most effectively from each other in a culture of collaboration and mutual accountability. Reflecting on professional practice tends to be more profitable when a colleague is able to help reflect on that practice, which in turn influences a choice of approaches.

6. **Change and development, for both the school community and its members, will be a steady, constant process rather than a dramatic, revolutionary reorientation.** One of the shortcomings of the early research on "effective schools" was that it tended to hold up models of such institutions as objects for emulation. If faculties could simply assume some of the properties of these schools, their institutions would be equally successful. What this early research did not show was how these schools came to be "effective."

The model for school development that we shall be exploring, and which is deeply rooted in the perspectives we have been discussing, is not a one-shot recipe for organizational success. It is a steady, gradual process by which a school community takes stock of itself and, step-by-step, seeks to improve the quality of its work.

Some writers have characterized this kind of development as focusing on means before ends (Sergiovanni 1996). In our experience, teachers commonly talk of how pleasantly surprised they were with the increase in student achievement. Their expectations had been wildly exceeded. Some talk of how a teaching episode changed quite dramatically as students interacted with the instructional material and with each other. Effective learning commonly occurs as the *ends* the teacher has in mind change as the *means* toward those ends develop. The goal is reached and surpassed, or more meaningful goals are substituted, or a successful experience leads to totally unexpected outcomes. Many of the approaches surveyed in this chapter, particularly Total Quality Management, are based on the idea that *ends* must be defined as a first step and teachers then simply need to uncover the *means* for achieving these goals. This is portrayed as a straight line process of "filling the gap."

The School Development approach begins with an emphasis on *means*. Before a school can consider improvements in student learning outcomes it must first focus on its culture, its beliefs, its values, and its shared understandings. Even when engaged with developing a school vision it is probably more important to have in place an effective process for discussing a possible vision than it is to reach an acceptable vision statement. The "final" statement may have a short currency.

It is the authors' view that effective schools are not correlated strongly with completed strategic plans but rather associated with the number and variety of opportunities that teachers have for sharing critical narrative about teaching and learning. The leadership that allows this to happen is often called *transformational*. This type of leadership is discussed in detail in Chapter 11.

Before a school can consider improvements in student learning outcomes it must first focus on its culture, its beliefs, its values, and its shared understandings.

A Fork in the Stream?

This chapter has discussed five contemporary movements in educational and management theory and attempted to show what these movements have in common. It should also be conceded that these movements differ one from another in many respects. One of the most interesting differences marks an important split in modern thinking about the way organizations work, or should work.

Twentieth century management theory has been based on the central notion that organizations are established to achieve goals. Effective organizations are therefore those that have clearly stated goals and well-defined processes for achieving these goals. The central importance of goals and goal-seeking behavior is implicit in most management theories, and quite explicit in approaches such as Total Quality Management and much of the literature on effective schools. In fact, viewing organizations as goal seeking is so central to most thinking about institutions that the validity or the usefulness of this concept is seldom questioned. Many of the theories surveyed in this chapter, and especially Total Quality Management, take as a given that the ends of any educational activity must be defined as the first and most important step, and that teachers simply need to execute the means for achieving these goals. The teaching task is depicted as one of defining the gap–between where the learner is and where the learner should be–and then filling that gap.

There is, however, an emerging stream of thought that holds that goals may not always be a useful focus for management efforts in educational institutions; that concentrating on process may be a more effective way of influencing the course of institutional development. What is meant by this claim?

Typically in schools, goals are seldom the powerful foci of effort that management theory would indicate. The goals of the school endure as the more or less predictable targets of excellence, effort, service, and fellowship. They serve to maintain the general direction of effort within the school, but do not always help to determine practice in the classroom or to resolve difficult choices facing teachers and administrators. An astute principal can justify almost any policy or practice by reference to one or more of the goals of the school, and just as readily produce a reason for not supporting any proposal by reference to another school goal.

The school culture movement has shown that this focus on goals may be misplaced in the case of most educational institutions. (Sergiovanni 1996). Researchers in this tradition have shown that more can be learned about where a school is going by examining what it is currently doing than by examining its goals. This same research tradition has illuminated another aspect of schooling that conflicts with the goal-directed model of organizational behavior–that the educative process is a creative interplay between teacher, subject matter, and learner, and that frequently the outcomes of the teaching and learning process will vastly exceed or widely vary from the intended outcomes. The intended goals will be reached and surpassed, or more meaningful goals will be substituted, or a successful learning experience will lead to a totally unexpected outcome. To deny the validity of this process is to misunderstand the nature of truly effective teaching. During effective teaching episodes it is common for the *ends* to change as the *means* develop.

What applies at the level of analysis also applies at the level of action. The key to effective teaching and learning is assisting teachers to reflect on what they are doing and trying to do in their instruction and the beliefs and values that underlie their actions. The key to effective school leadership is to develop and sustain a school culture that encourages and supports teachers in this process of reflection, redefinition, and change. In such a culture the faculty and principal *discover the goals*, that is the *ends*, of their endeavors as they reflect on what they are doing and what they believe.

This emphasis on means rather than ends is a central one for the School Development approach that is being discussed in this book. This approach may seem strange to anyone deeply versed in a goals approach to school leadership. Most principals will find it hard to believe that

More can be learned about where a school is going by examining what it is currently doing than by examining its goals.

school effectiveness is likely to correlate more strongly with the number and variety of opportunities that teachers have for sharing critical narrative about teaching and learning than it does with well-prepared strategic plans. This, too, is associated with transformational leadership—a style that allows for this critical exchange about teaching practice is discussed in depth in the final chapter.

As with most theories about human behavior and interaction, this refocusing on means rather than goals is just as capable of overstatement and error as the goal-focused hegemony that it seeks to displace. It would be foolish to claim there is no place for goal-directed activities in schools. Some of the most promising innovations under way in American schools today owe their success to their clear goals and to the rigor with which those goals infuse every aspect of practice. While the principal focus of this book will be on means rather than ends, it will be important to show how this perspective on management can support and promote practices with an equally strong goal focus.

A School Development Framework

We now have some directions for school development. We have seen that several of the most important lines of contemporary research on education and management have identified some common themes and directions. In the previous section several of these following points of agreement have been identified:

- learning requires the individual to actively construct meaning and knowledge on the basis of reflecting upon experience;
- at an organizational level this view of learning requires members of a school community to

gather data systematically on the key processes they are endeavoring to develop and to reflect collectively on the significance of that data;
- the primary objective for the principal is to establish a learning community;
- the principal has a critical role in upholding the mission of the school and ensuring that the establishment of the learning community becomes the major preoccupation for all members of the school community;
- the development of a culture of collaboration and mutual accountability is a necessary step on the path to that learning community;
- change and development for both the school community and its members will be a steady, constant process rather than a dramatic, revolutionary reorientation.

These points of agreement constitute a useful start for a principal or a school community wishing to become more effective. They point out a direction for development, and they suggest a philosophy and a style of leadership. But, as they are, they fall short of an action agenda for a school leadership that really wishes to accomplish change.

The research literature is full of examples and models of effective practice. The qualities of the "effective school" have been known and repeatedly verified for the past two decades. For example, it is known that schools with:

- a clear mission;
- a collegial and participative style of management;
- an emphasis on learning outcomes and classroom practice;
- a strong learning culture

will be more effective than schools lacking these qualities. It is also known that probably the ma-

One of the reasons so many schools are unable to emulate the achievements of more effective institutions is that they do not know how to move from their present state of affairs to the desired state.

jority of schools fall short on several of these qualities despite the best efforts of principals and teachers.

One of the reasons so many schools are unable to emulate the achievements of more effective institutions is that they do not know how to move from their present state of affairs to the desired state. To be told to emulate a model without being told how is like being told to drive to a remote city without being given directions or a map. It is one thing to acknowledge that effective schools exhibit a collaborative style of management; it is altogether another to know how to develop such a style in one's own institution. Or, one can readily agree that teachers who regularly reflect on their professional practice will become more effective, and yet be totally at a loss as to how to encourage such reflection. A daunting feature of the "effective schools" literature is that the schools they describe as case studies tend to be so different from one's own. A school with a farsighted principal, a community that is thoroughly involved in the life of the institution, and a teaching force that is constantly focused on classroom processes and learning outcomes can hardly fail to produce the desired results, but how does one ever get to this happy state of affairs?

In the previous section some goals were identified for school development—or some destinations, to use the driving analogy. The remainder of the book will draw some maps and suggest some directions to help schools get to these destinations. Or, if the driving analogy suggests a line of direction that is altogether too linear and limited, some tools will be discussed that a school can use to help it develop the institutional model it wants.

A school is a complex organization with a lot of processes going on at the same time. If principals hope to change that organization and to move it in some of the directions that we have described, they shall need to be working on more than one level at a time, and in more than one area. The sheer complexity of the development challenge may be one of the reasons why so many principals are unable to emulate the "effective school"–they simply do not know where to begin in the process. But when confronted with complexity it is usually a good idea to see whether a process can be reduced to a number of simpler components. This may suggest an appropriate sequence for developing each component. It may even allow some specialization of effort within the organization so that everyone does not have to be working on everything at the same time. This is the approach that shall be taken in the remainder of this book.

In attempting to break down the challenge of School Development into simpler and more manageable components, following are at least two dimensions on which this division can be made:

- First, it may be possible to draw a distinction between individual members of the school community and the community as a whole– between the *individual* and the *school;* this is a useful distinction to draw as there is likely to be a continual tension between the needs of the individual child, parent, teacher, or principal and the needs of the collective as a school moves toward a more participative style of management. The demands of collaboration will require an emphasis on the group, and the development of group skills and a collective culture. This will require a major and sustained investment of effort by the whole school community. But if this group development process is to succeed, it cannot be at the expense of the individual members of the school community. Care needs to be taken that there is a place for the individual in this strengthening group culture.
- The second dimension may be less obvious but no less important. School Development has a commitment to both *development* and *ap-*

praisal. "Development" refers to the growth and advancement of the school, its members, its policies, and its practices. "Appraisal" refers to the requirement for everyone within a school community to be accountable for what they are doing, and for all processes, policies, and programs to be subject to regular appraisal and assessment to determine their effectiveness.

The juxtaposition of these two processes of development and appraisal has always posed a difficulty for school leadership. History suggests that principals cannot easily discharge both responsibilities at the same time. If they strenuously execute their responsibility to appraise and report, then their staff will be reluctant to engage in risk-taking developmental activities, particularly where administrators are closely involved. If the principal is to discharge both responsibilities with equal effect then great care must be taken to maintain a distinction between the two processes and to communicate that distinction with great clarity to all concerned. The distinction is so important that it needs to be treated as an organizing principle for the entire School Development strategy.

The operation of these two dimensions can be expressed in the form of a matrix with the School and the Individual along one axis, and Development and Appraisal along the other. The four quadrants on this matrix each represent a different focus for School Development (Matrix II on following page).

This matrix provides a framework for the rest of the book. Part II examines a sequence for School Development—data gathering, collaborative analysis of the data, structural change, and a focus on teaching and learning. Part III concerns individual development and two approaches found to be useful and consistent with the key points drawn from previous discussion—Quality

	School	Individual
Development	*Quadrant 1* *Four Phases of School Development* • Data collection • Collaboration • Structural change • Focus on teaching and learning	*Quadrant 2* *Principals and teachers engaging in reflective thought through:* • Quality Learning Circles • Thematic Supervision • Professional development and support beyond the school
Appraisal	*Quadrant 3* *School Review and Principal Appraisal* • Conceptual Job Description for the principal • Regular appraisal of the principal • Thematic review of the school	*Quadrant 4* *Teacher Appraisal* • Conceptual Job Description for all teachers • Professional Development Consultation cycle

Matrix II: Structure of *The Reflective Principal*

Learning Circles and Thematic Supervision. Part IV discusses appraisal. In this section principal—and through the principal, school appraisal—and teacher appraisal are examined. Part V integrates the issues and activities covered in each of the four quadrants and shows how the developmental process can be implemented through the course of the school year.

Part II

The Process of
School Development

Part II

The Process of School Development

Theory that helps school principals think about their jobs is a good theory. One that helps them select an appropriate course of action is an even better one. In the previous section a number of theories were examined that may help school leaders reflect on their work in a constructive and analytical way. This ability to analyze and reflect is of little value, however, if administrators do not also have the ability to move from reflection to action. If effective action follows from careful reflection and analysis, the same principle applies to the school as a whole. Effective action by a faculty tends to be made on the basis of shared reflection and analysis. School Development is the process by which a school develops this capacity for reflective action.

The Critically Reflective Process

This book is titled *The Reflective Principal* because the literature suggests that a critically reflective process offers the best opportunity for school leaders to fashion meaningful schools. Being reflective, in this sense, means that princi-

71

pals will examine and uncover their own assumptions about teaching and how schools work, while at the same time providing the space and conditions for the same process to operate widely within the school community (Brookfield 1995).

The critically reflective process is more than simply thinking about events that have passed. Reflection is the ability to draw links between thinking and action on the one hand and an understanding of "what made me this way" on the other. Stephen Brookfield describes the process of identifying these links as "hunting assumptions" (1995, 2). This process may begin by bringing these underlying assumptions to the surface, but there is also a need to talk about them and their effects with colleagues. A School Development process may begin with individual reflection but, to be successful, will need to move swiftly to a shared, collaborative mode. The following example may illustrate this sequence:

- Principals may reflect on incidents of disruptive student behavior that have been raised by members of the faculty. They could then write down some of the assumptions about appropriate behavior and how they believe the faculty should respond to these incidents. This process of individual reflection starts to be transformed into School Development as principals involve faculty in thinking and talking about these incidents.
- It may be necessary for groups of teachers to gather first-hand data about student behavior that they would classify as "disruptive." They will then relate these events and their context to their colleagues and share their thinking and reactions about them. Such discussions can be defined as "critical reflection" when assumptions underlying these actions are revealed and clarified and energy is applied to creating a range of alternative actions. This process encourages individuals to draw connec-

tions and links between their attitudes and responses on the one hand and the core values that sustain the integrity of their actions on the other. The group as a whole begins to understand and appreciate the diversity of the core values represented among their number.

Group reflection takes time, of course. Principals need to consider with some care the issues they will treat in this way. Before allocating time and resources to collaborative reflection it is necessary to ensure that there is:

- agreement among faculty about the existence and importance of the issue to be addressed;
- a commitment from the faculty (and possibly the community or students) to spending time focused on this issue;
- the allocation of sufficient resources of time and money;
- the willingness of the organization to consider any structural or technical changes necessary to resolve the issue;
- willingness to abandon the planned change and recommit the school to a renewed search for alternatives if the agreed change failed to solve the original problem.

A commitment to collaborative reflection by a principal and teachers will not be enough to ensure that this process becomes a regular feature of school life, or that this commitment endures. In a sense School Development helps a school community to plan an evolving sequence of collaborative reflection. This will start at a level at which faculty are comfortable and progress to more challenging activities as the confidence and understanding of teachers grow.

Chapter 3

A Sequence for School Development

One of the most difficult challenges facing a school attempting to become more effective is getting the School Development process started. Many principals have made a personal commitment to address a significant organizational problem by adopting a more collaborative management style, yet failed miserably in their first attempts. Others begin by introducing a structural solution to a particular problem. Often this solution is imported from another setting, and just as often the "solution" is rejected by the school community. Or alternatively they assume a far greater level of consensus and shared values among the staff than is the case, and subsequently find their initiative fails for want of support.

Generally these principals are attempting to go too far and too fast. Collaboration and consensus building cannot be taken for granted, and their successful achievement tends to be a necessary prerequisite of change rather than a felicitous by-product. If major innovations are to be implemented successfully in schools they need to be preceded by developmental activities that establish the technical skills required for cooperative action, which build up the level of trust and collegiality within the staff. In short, it seems

Collaboration and consensus building cannot be taken for granted, and their successful achievement tends to be a necessary prerequisite of change rather than a felicitous by-product.

that certain types of developmental activities must come before others if the latter are to be successful. Research and observation over more than a decade suggest that there may be a general sequence for School Development, a sequence that any school could follow with some confidence (Prebble and Stewart 1981; Stewart and Prebble 1985). The suggested sequence has four phases of development activities.

Phase 1. Understanding the School Culture through Data Gathering

The first step in the School Development process is for the teachers to develop an understanding of the interrelationships between the faculty and the functioning of the school. Before the school can embark on any ambitious problem-solving or collaborative action, it is important that people know how the system works right now. Teachers need to develop a sense of collective awareness, and this is best achieved through systematic data gathering and feedback by the faculty members themselves. Increasingly this process will also involve the parent community. As the circle of consultation grows wider it becomes increasingly important to take the time to understand the school culture before attempting to change it.

Phase 2. Collaborative Analysis and Problem Solving

Activities in Phase 1 will have identified and clarified a number of organizational problems. The next step in the process is for members of the school community to work together to solve these problems. This kind of intensive faculty participation may be a new experience for many school communities, in which case the members will need to learn to work collaboratively. They will need to learn when and how to reach consensus decisions; to expect conflict and know when it needs to be resolved and how to resolve it; they will need to recognize and value the plurality of values and talents represented among their number; they will need to pay more explicit attention to the way they communicate within group settings; and they will need to identify collective goals while recognizing the desirability of allowing individual members to interpret these goals in idiosyncratic ways.

Phase 3. Structural Change

As the community gains a heightened perception of the way the school operates as an organization, and as the faculty comes to experience greater participation in decision making and policy formation, it is likely that certain structural changes will be needed to accommodate these changes. Most schools are organized on the basis of limited collective decision making. As teachers renegotiate collective goals and come to accept a greater sense of mutual accountability, it is likely that the existing patterns of school organization will need to be changed to accommodate this shift of organizational culture. These structural changes, when they come, will be a natural expression of an emerging, developing school culture rather than the cause of opposition among a poorly prepared faculty group.

Phase 4. A Focus on Teaching and Learning

The point of the previous three phases is to bring the school to the stage when it can focus its

The basis of collaborative reflection and action is knowledge: about the school; about other people's perception of the school; and about the ways in which the school works and does not work.

attention more directly on the key tasks of the institution–helping students to learn. If the members of the school have come to an improved understanding of the way the school operates, if they have learned how to work together to solve institutional problems, and if they have been able to introduce structures that are more appropriate to the job at hand, then it is likely that teachers will be able to devote attention more energetically to the challenges of improving the quality of teaching and learning and the impact on student achievement.

These phases are not merely arbitrary divisions made in an otherwise undifferentiated process. They serve as a useful guide for schools wishing to embark on a sustained attempt to boost their effectiveness through collaborative action. The basis of collaborative reflection and action is knowledge: about the school; about other people's perception of the school; and about the ways in which the school works and does not work.

As the members of a school community begin to gather data about the school process and to discuss the implications of those data among themselves, they begin to establish a kind of corporate awareness. Problems that were previously understood by only a handful of teachers become acknowledged by everyone. This is a vital first step if any sustained corporate action is to take place at a later date. Such action will be on that basis of shared understandings and critical reflection.

There is also a more pragmatic and political reason for beginning the School Development process with data gathering. This activity is the least threatening form of collective action in which teachers can be asked to engage. Almost any change can be interpreted as dangerous and threatening by some teachers. Changes affecting classroom practice are usually seen as most threatening of all as they touch on teachers' core professional values. But changes in school organization, routines, traditions, or symbols can be resisted equally strongly if teachers fail to understand and accept the benefits of the changes. However, even conservative faculties will see the sense in learning more about how the school operates.

As teachers engage in this first phase of collective data gathering–analysis and discussion–they are thrown into collaborative working relationships. Often their previous professional experience has provided little training in working closely with other faculty members. Most teachers' days are spent in isolation from their peers. Group work with students may not translate easily to working relationships with colleagues. It cannot be taken for granted that teachers have the required level of skills in collective decision making. However, it is possible to monitor this phase of collaborative problem solving and to help them to recognize and learn the sorts of skills they will need for collaborative action. There is no point in helping a faculty to work together collectively before those teachers have begun to look at the state of the organization. Teachers will only accept this sort of guidance and help when they see that it is needed and in the service of a shared objective.

Once the faculty has begun to work together in a more collaborative manner it is likely that some structural changes will be necessary to accommodate these new working relationships. Such structural changes should arise out of a shift to a more collaborative work culture, rather than the reverse. Schools are littered with malfunctioning structural arrangements introduced to encourage a new type of working relationship between teachers and students, but failed because the need for the new relationship was never accepted by teachers, or else only partially understood by them. Collaborative problem solving leads naturally to generating structural solu-

Teachers need the support and guidance of a group of colleagues who know where they are going, and who share some commitment to help each other to get there.

tions. Again, it is the role of the principal to promote the habit of working collaboratively toward these changes.

The final emphasis on curriculum and program change has a certain internal logic to it. It is only when a school community understands the way the organization currently operates, has taken steps to identify and solve organizational problems on a collective basis, and has set up structures to facilitate collaborative working relationships that teachers will have the support they need to make significant improvements to the teaching programs within their classrooms. However, this phase of the School Development cycle relates more to the ability of the school community as a whole to focus on classroom programs rather than the ability of individual teachers to improve the quality of their classroom teaching.

It is commonly acknowledged that most teachers do not teach nearly as well as they know how to, or use more than a fraction of the knowledge about teaching and learning that they possess. Teachers do not need a constant torrent of new ideas and techniques from outside the school. They need instead the support and guidance of a group of colleagues who know where they are going, and who share some commitment to help each other to get there.

When the faculty of a school have reached the fourth phase, they can all focus on the primary purpose of the school–helping students to learn. The faculty's accomplishments would already be considerable. Its members would have the following:

- access to a wide range of process skills;
- well-developed expectations and methods of faculty participation and collaboration;
- the ability to focus increasingly on program evaluation and curriculum development, made easier by the use of flexible meeting proce-

dures, teachers interacting across the whole school, less experienced teachers being given opportunities to lead, and everyone being comfortable with collaborative data gathering and feedback;
* reliable and regular feedback about how they are doing and support that is readily available in the event of a crisis at the classroom level;
* a school community that is taking responsibility for its own development.

In addition:

* the principal has well-developed structures for obtaining additional information and methods of supervision that are efficient and accepted;
* the school, its fund of knowledge and expertise, as well as its buildings and physical facilities, can become available as a learning resource for the whole community.

The Importance of Beginning with Data Gathering

School Development is based on the assumption that an effective school is impossible without high-quality information. Just as a principal needs information before taking unilateral action, so the school as a whole needs a great deal of information before reaching a collaborative decision on a complex issue. It seems to be the case that the greater the level of participation that is sought, the more data that are needed to ensure an acceptable and effective solution. Data gathering and analysis are important stages between the identification of a problem and the selection and implementation of a solution. Data gathering allows the school to reach an informed decision; it allows the faculty to learn more about a problem and the school generally; it increases

Each member of a school is constantly engaged in an effort to construct his or her theory-in-use of the school.

the commitment of the staff to finding a solution and sticking to it; and it may prevent a faculty from embarking on needless change. But more importantly, collaborative data gathering is an important way in which a faculty can learn.

The aim of School Development is to help the school as a whole become more effective by learning about itself. A school does not make decisions and behave like an individual. Individuals take action on the basis of implicit theories they have about the nature of reality and the anticipated consequences of that action. Chris Argyris and Donald Schön (1978) suggest that these theories-of-action can be discovered in two ways. People can be asked how they behave in specific circumstances and why, or else the implicit theory can be deduced by observing them in action. Asking a person how he or she behaves, we will be told the individual's "espoused theory," which may bear little relationship to the "theory-in-use" we deduce from observing an individual's actual behavior.

Individuals learn when they are forced to change their implicit theories, either theories-in-use or espoused theories, when they accommodate a new reality, or more particularly, when they are forced to reconcile their theories-in-use with their espoused theories. Argyris and Schön suggest that we cannot assume that a school learns in the same way. "Schools" only learn, remember, and think in a metaphorical sense. Schools do these things through the independent actions of their members. Schools certainly do have espoused theories that are claimed to govern the way their members take action. Written role descriptions, local or state mandates, and policy statements would all be examples of espoused theories. However, as with individual action, such espoused theories may not be accurate guides to interpreting organizational behavior. Instead, each member of a school is constantly engaged in an effort to construct his or her theory-in-use of the school. Everyone is endeavoring to know "how things get done around here," and to improve their representation or image of the theory-in-use of the school. Of course, there is no abstract, overarching organizational theory-in-use to be found. There is nothing more than the combination of all the members' theories-in-use of the school. This has no greater reality than the shared descriptions and explanations that individual members jointly construct and that guide their thinking and action within the school.

As individual members modify their images of the school and the ways in which it operates, so the organizational theory-in-use gradually shifts—but only gradually. If genuine organizational learning is to take place, new theories and explanations must be understood by all members of the school. If a school's theory-in-use is to alter significantly it is not sufficient for the principal or even a small leadership team to have a new image of the school. The whole faculty must come to share this new explanation and direction. The key to this kind of organizational learning is collective data gathering, analysis, and feedback. Organizational learning permeates all four phases of School Development. While the first phase explicitly emphasizes data gathering and feedback, the other three phases maintain a strong questioning and reflective posture. Each of the phases can be seen as an attempt to find answers to different sorts of questions.

Phase 1. How Do Things Work Around Here?

While there are many directions this original data gathering could take, in practice schools tend to concentrate on communications, influence, and control. For example, the following questions are commonly asked:

- How is information disseminated in this school?
- Who makes the important decisions?
- How are decisions changed?
- How is school policy arrived at?
- Who is in control of critical resources, and how do they exercise this responsibility?
- How are collective decisions made and meeting procedures organized?
- Who makes the important decisions affecting faculty (i.e., teacher duties), and on what basis?

Phase 2. Can We Start to Look at Our Problems Together?

As people start to work collaboratively, the following sorts of questions may be asked about the processes of collective action:

- When should teachers be involved in executive decision making?
- How do we go about reaching a consensus on a complex issue?
- Are faculty meetings a good use of our time?
- Is information disseminated rapidly and effectively?
- How should we discuss the goals of the school or the curriculum?
- How should we handle conflict among the staff?
- Are there problems in understanding other points of view?
- Is the work load shared equitably?
- Are people getting their needs met by the school?

Phase 3. Will We Need to Make Changes in the Way the School is Organized?

As teachers overcome some of their initial inhibitions about working together, they are likely to begin to ask questions with implications for structural change:

- Does the school give teachers the kind of support they need and want?
- What purpose does the present team or departmental structure serve?
- Do members of the faculty and those with significant delegated duties get reasonable access to the principal?
- Are there better ways to organize our collective decision making in terms of meetings?
- Does the schedule facilitate or hinder the kinds of working relationships we wish to develop?
- Is it possible to supply supervising teachers with more release time to allow them to assist the members of their team?
- Do some of the roles and responsibilities of teachers need to be redefined?

Phase 4. Are We Now Able to Concentrate on Teaching and Learning?

Apart from those in newly established schools, few principals ever find themselves in the position to start afresh. There is always a program in action, whatever its worth. Consequently, Phase 4 often begins with a foray into the field of classroom practice. Questions pertaining to classroom practice that might be asked include the following:

- What assessment is made of a student's prior learning?
- How is this assessment information evaluated in planning instruction?
- What kinds of learning resources and learning experiences are planned for?
- How are instructional approaches matched to learning needs?

Experience suggests that teachers seldom collect data systematically for the purpose of instructional evaluation.

- Is the best use being made of instructional time?
- Is the classroom managed and organized effectively as a learning environment?

Experience suggests that teachers seldom collect data systematically for the purpose of instructional evaluation (that is, assessment data upon which instructional decisions are based). Consequently there is a tendency to use the assessment data gathered as a summative evaluation, summarizing the learning as an end point of the process. School Development, however, is grounded on the principle that data are about formative evaluation–assessment data that "inform" the teacher at the classroom level about the next steps for student learning and at the school level about key issues in school development. Data are vital ingredients in all decisions that are made in the school.

A Culture of Collaboration

School Development is not some value-neutral technique that can be applied to any managerial objective. It is a value-explicit strategy intended to influence schools in quite definite ways. One of the most important School Development values is that of collaboration. "Collaboration" means a cooperative venture based on shared power and authority. This is not to go as far as some theorists, who would insist that hierarchy is incompatible with collaboration (Kraus 1980, 19), but a School Development approach does make the assumption that most schools are unlikely to become more effective unless they move toward a culture of collaboration.

The structures and processes of collaborative management do not concern us at this point, except to say that School Development is a process intended to assist schools in becoming more genuinely collaborative. Some of these processes are examined in more detail in Appendix A. Of interest at this point are the values and assumptions that underlie this major commitment to collaboration. In a fuller treatment of this topic, William Kraus identifies nineteen sub-values of collaboration (1980, 130). The next section examines five of the more important of Kraus's list, and adds a sixth.

Values and Assumptions that Underlie Collaboration

There are certain values and assumptions that underlie collaboration in any organization.

1. Pluralism

Pluralism is the recognition that members of a school are likely to adhere to differing values from one another, and that the well-being of the school owes as much to the differences between these values as it does to the similarities. Individuals need not lose their identity in the school, but schools are more than simply the sum of their individual members. A collaborative management strategy will allow the school to negotiate and strive for collective objectives while at the same time recognizing the needs of individual members. A related notion that reinforces the desirability of shared decision making is the concept of the "variety pool." If the leadership of a school excludes all but administrators from executive decision making it is probable that over time this decision making will become stereotyped and predictable. The variety pool from which alternative courses of action are drawn will be relatively small. If, on the other hand, more faculty are asked to share in discussing the problem and suggesting solutions, the variety pool is expanded exponentially.

In most schools, problem solving is not a highly valued or frequent activity.

2. Power Generation

"Power," "control," or "influence"–whichever word we choose to use–should be seen as a necessary ingredient for organizational effectiveness, and not automatically dismissed as an undesirable feature. In collaborative schools where people are committed to working collectively toward shared goals, it is very important that people exercise influence over each other. The acceptance of the idea of collective responsibility implies an acceptance of the obligation to negotiate the ends, as well as the means, of collective action within a school. Members of a school faculty must be prepared not only to influence their colleagues in the values they hold and the ways in which those values are worked out in action, but also be prepared to accept their colleagues' attempts to influence them. This is a most important idea, and one developed in more detail later.

3. Problem Solving and Problem Finding

As already stated, School Development is a strategy for helping schools to identify and solve their important problems and challenges. This assertion does not seem very remarkable until faculties are reminded that, in most schools, problem solving is not a highly valued or frequent activity. The political and bureaucratic forces influencing many schools frequently inhibit members from attempting to push for organizational solutions. There is a defensiveness, an inertia, and sometimes even a positive antagonism to the idea of collective problem solving. There may also be an impatience with the deliberate, step-by-step process required in collective problem solving, as influential members of the school push for their own favored solutions.

4. Participation

The value of encouraging participation in organizational decision making can be argued for its own sake. In a democratic society, there is as strong a case for involving people in the important decisions affecting their work life as there is for allowing them a say in the direction of public affairs. In addition to this basic argument, participation does result in a greater level of commitment and identification with the enterprise in which the individual is engaged. In a people-centered activity such as teaching it would seem particularly important that a school community should not become alienated from the task society asks them to perform.

5. Consensus

Collaborative action is normally dependent on a consensus among the members of a school. Consensus is generally misinterpreted to mean that everyone is in total agreement on an issue. Such agreement is usually only possible on trivial matters, and clearly could not form the basis of any genuinely collaborative leadership style. There is another, more useful operational definition of consensus. Consensus, according to this second definition, implies that an issue has been explored thoroughly, that the arguments for and against various courses of action have been debated fully, and that finally, all the members of the school are prepared to abide by the best available solution. Consensus decision making does not therefore completely remove the possibility of conflict. The important requirement is that, in spite of their misgivings, members of a faculty should agree not to sabotage a consensus agreement for the course of the agreement. If this seems an unreasonable expectation of someone whose ideas have been rejected by the majority, there should be a definite life to any such agreement. One of the reasons teachers may be unwilling to commit themselves to proposed innovations and organizational changes is that they are aware that such a commitment is usually irreversible. Innovations may drag on for years but are doomed to fail, and evaluations are promised but never take place. Genuine consensus decision making should extract an undertaking of support (or at the very least, nonsabotage) from all members of the school, but in exchange, should indicate quite specifically how the innovation will be evaluated, and the date by which the innovation should have been established as a success, modified, or abandoned.

6. Interdependence and Mutual Accountability

The value of interdependence is of paramount importance to a successful School Development initiative. Most importantly, the values themselves are interdependent. Collective problem solving will only work if the value of pluralism is respected. Power generation will only be tolerated if the values of participation and consensus are pursued equally vigorously. Collective ends are only achievable if the leadership understands and respects the commitment and motivation of individual members of the school.

What is needed is a form of "negotiated order" in which the various interests represented within the school are acknowledged as legitimate. Subsumed under this value of interdependence is the value of mutual accountability. Engaged as they are on a corporate task, teachers and administrators should expect, and be given, the opportunity to justify their beliefs and their practice to one another, and to influence one another. This value may be at odds with some interpretations of "professional autonomy"–a term often used to shield teachers from the legitimate influence of their colleagues and to absolve them from any responsibility for the work of these same colleagues.

A Process, Not a Product

It was stressed at the beginning of this book that individual schools are in the best position to identify their own needs and problems, and to come up with their own solutions. What is proposed as School Development is a *process* that schools may find useful in working their way through to their own solutions. Having said this, it is very difficult to discuss a process at any length without providing some examples of the kind of solutions that may result. Later in this book processes such as Quality Learning Circles and Thematic Supervision are described. In a sense these processes are answers to someone else's problem. Schools are cautioned against "buying" such a product "off the shelf." If any of these techniques and processes are to work in another school, they should be solutions arrived at by the faculty as part of continuing School Development. It is only when the faculty has spent time getting to understand how the school works and started to work collaboratively to identify and solve some of the significant challenges facing their organization that the school is in any position to consider major structural changes such as these.

School Development is a strategy that helps faculties through a process of critical reflection to clarify why they think as they do and identify those practices and procedures that best promote

Individual schools are in the best position to identify their own needs and problems, and to come up with their own solutions.

A key role for the principal through a School Development cycle will be as a process facilitator, keeping the group on task, pointing the way ahead, and helping teachers to develop and practice the necessary skills of data gathering and group interaction.

quality teaching and learning. Once identified, they become embedded as school policies and legitimated as "the way things work around here." There is greater commitment and more energy when teachers find that classroom practices they have developed themselves are confirmed by the school leadership. In a collaborative environment, new practices will inevitably be subject to rigorous scrutiny both by the administrators and their teacher colleagues. If they pass the test and gain acceptance, credit flows to the initiating teachers recognized as professionals who are keen to use their own intellect to devise and adapt to new ways of teaching and learning.

The Role of the Principal

A cycle of activities has been described for assisting a school community to develop the capacity for reflective action. What is the role of the principal in this process? This will be a recurring theme, and one that will be taken up in each chapter throughout this book. For the moment, three roles will be proposed. These are not suggested as a complete or definitive statement of the principal's contribution to the School Development process. They are advanced at this point more to indicate the very different functions that this process will call on the principal to perform.

The Principal as Process Facilitator

A key role for the principal through a School Development cycle will be as a process facilitator, keeping the group on task, pointing the way ahead, and helping teachers to develop and practice the necessary skills of data gathering and group interaction. Learning how to gather and analyze data on perceived problems within the school may be a new challenge for many teachers. The faculty might decide, for example, to commence a cycle of development activities by carrying out a survey of teacher expectations. What do teachers think the school expects of them this year, and what do they expect of the school? The principal will need to make time and other support resources available for this survey to be carried out. It will be important that the teachers themselves carry out the survey to ensure that the data are seen to be authentic, and that they have some sense of ownership and commitment to the results. The principal may also need to guide the data gathering process itself, suggesting perhaps that the survey should remain anonymous to encourage full and frank participation by all teachers. The principal will also want to work with the faculty to establish protocols about how the data will be analyzed and how they intend to cope with widely different statements that such an exercise is likely to elicit.

The Principal as Collector of Artifacts

School Development is a process that works on and within the culture of the school. The principal has an important role in drawing the links that can be identified between the leadership and organization of the school on the one hand, with the values, beliefs, aspirations, and taken-for-granted assumptions that members of the school community have on the other. One powerful way in which the principal can demonstrate these links is by collecting and displaying significant cultural "artifacts" to the school community. In this sense, artifacts would be observed behaviors in the life of the school that supported or detracted from the current stated core values the school purported to follow. In the same way that archaeologists gain an understanding of what previous

Thinking about the school as a learning community rather than as a tool or an organization will suggest a different sort of role for the principal than the usual one of manager or boss.

civilizations held to be important by an examination of their artifacts, school communities can gain useful understanding of what is genuinely valued by examining what is actually done. One particularly powerful way of doing this is by documenting those behaviors and systems that are unique to the school.

The Principal as Community Developer

What principals do, and how they spend their time, will depend to a very large extent on how they think about the school and their role within it. In Chapter 1 reference was made to Phillip Schlechty's (1990) notion that the way leaders "conceptualize the purpose of their enterprise will, in the long run, shape the way their organizations are envisioned and structured." Thinking about the school as a learning community rather than as a tool or an organization will suggest a different sort of role for the principal than the usual one of manager or boss. This role will be that of community developer. A community is sustained by the commitment of its citizens. A community developer has to retain excitement and commitment among the citizenry if they are to work toward any shared goals. This sort of commitment cannot be mandated, nor will it arise through line-staff performance appraisals where meeting a range of mandated competencies takes precedence.

Teachers need time and opportunity to reflect with their colleagues about their professional practice. It is this talking and learning from each other that will illuminate best practices, encourage diversity, and engender a sense of community. Given structured opportunities to discuss important themes, groups of teachers begin to recognize a sense of community and shared commitment. The reflective principal will build on these new relationships and share supportive ideas from the literature to help the faculty understand the processes of change and development in new ways. What begins to emerge is a school that is "culturally tight and managerially loose" (Weick 1976).

A school that shares these characteristics can result from the process of School Development that is the central theme of this book. At the beginning of this chapter it was noted that one of the most challenging aspects of any school development is getting the process started. The next chapter sets out in more detail how School Development can be initiated and sustained through the four-phase developmental process of data gathering, collaborative analysis, structural change, and focusing on teaching and learning.

Chapter 4

Four Phases of School Development

This chapter sets out in more detail key aspects of the School Development process. In Chapter 2, two key dimensions of the School Development process were identified and expressed in the form of a matrix. The first dimension concerns the *individual* and the *school*, and the second, *development* and *appraisal*. Each of the four quadrants represents a different focus for School Development. In this chapter, the focus is on the school as an organization. While it may seem unusual to consider the school development process before that of the individuals who comprise it, the reason is sound. There is considerable advantage in the school making some progress toward developing a new focus and cultural perspective first, then putting its energies into the personal and professional development of its members. It is also well to remember that becoming involved in the school's organizational development is itself an important part of an individual member's personal and professional growth.

Phase 1. Data Gathering

When a school community considers a problem that its members have identified, there is a

97

If the basis for action within a school is the understanding that teachers and students have about their work, then the only way that significant change will ever take place is if all members have the opportunity to reflect on and modify that understanding.

natural and laudable tendency to look immediately for a solution. Similarly, when new principals take over schools they are likely to have many bright new ideas they would like to see put into action. Astute principals can often identify changes that are needed within just a few hours. Why then is it necessary to delay while the faculty engages in a protracted exercise in data gathering?

The simple answer to this question is that when innovations are imposed on schools they almost always fail. Research studies into educational innovations have come up with a number of explanations for this failure, including the following:

- educational systems seem to be inherently conservative;
- schools possess a high level of inertia;
- teachers have developed the practice of passive sabotage to a high art form;
- unanticipated consequences always seem to jeopardize the change effort;
- it is extremely difficult to verify or demonstrate the effectiveness of many educational innovations.

A more convincing explanation lies at the heart of our understanding of organizations and their life and culture. Tom Greenfield (Macpherson 1984) has reminded educational administrators that schools are no more than an invented social reality. Teachers, students, and administrators all bring their own beliefs, values, and wills to the school and together construct a system of shared meanings, moral order, and power. These shared understandings certainly influence the behavior of members of the organization, but they have no objective reality outside the minds of the members. If the basis for action within a school is the understanding that teachers and students have about their work, then the only way that significant change will ever take place is if all members have the opportunity to reflect on and modify that understanding. Greenfield claims that "much of our action as individuals in organizations is unaware action. We simply have been programmed into it in some way" (Macpherson 1984, 4). In order to change their practice, people must change their understanding. In order to change their understanding, they need to be aware of what they are doing and why. The most straightforward way they can become aware of their practice is to gather data about what they are doing and to argue about its meaning with their colleagues.

Phase 1 in the School Development program is a commitment to data gathering, reflection, and dialogue. We have talked already about the need for collaboration in School Development and the need for a norm of mutual accountability among a faculty. However, collaboration and mutual accountability are impossible unless members of the organization are able to debate their values and practices on a regular basis. Collaboration is no better than tyranny if teachers are never given the chance to challenge the directions of school policy. And mutual accountability quickly reverts to top-down supervision if the essential features of the school program remain nonnegotiable. Before a "solution" is imposed on a school there must be a process of reflection about the nature of the "problem." What looks like a problem to one group of teachers may not be to another group. These differences of opinion and perception need to be identified and negotiated before an administrator commits the school to a far-reaching program of change. The basis of collaborative action is a belief that corporate action should be based on shared norms and understandings, rather than on selective knowledge, hierarchical influence, and coercive power. The

*The vital thing
is to develop
the habit of
data gathering
within the
faculty.*

starting point for those shared norms and understandings is shared data about the essential features of corporate life.

There is another more practical reason why
data gathering should precede any of the other
phases of School Development. As noted, it is the
least threatening form of collective action teachers can undertake. Data gathering makes few assumptions about the nature of problems facing
the school, the competing educational and political ideologies represented within the school, and
the level of agreement among teachers and the
parent community about the existing programs
or goals of the school. It simply challenges the
teachers to look at what is happening in the
school right now, to gather data in a careful and
objective manner, and to debate the significance
of those data among themselves. It is a procedure
that can scarcely be resisted by even the most
hidebound teacher, as no further action is implied by merely gathering data and talking about
them. It is also a procedure that should reassure
teachers that the direction of the School Development process lies as much in their hands as in
the principal's.

What Do We Collect Data About?

This question may seem absolutely fundamental to this first stage of data gathering. How
can a faculty proceed very far in data gathering if
they are not sure of the object of their inquiry? In
fact the focus of the initial data gathering exercise may be less important than the fact that the
school is engaged in this collaborative process together. The vital thing is to develop the habit of
data gathering within the faculty, and to increase
their collective knowledge and understanding
about important organizational procedures and
problems. Data may be gathered on an almost in-

finite number of phenomena within a school, but it may be helpful to think of the following three broad levels of data gathering:

- The first level of data gathering is to consider the school as a totality and to gather information about a wide number of organizational processes. Because of its great breadth of focus, this kind of approach will either be necessarily superficial, or else time-consuming and expensive. The whole of a school's faculty, and possibly also the community and the student body, will be involved in gathering, analyzing, and debating the data that are collected in such an exercise.
- The second level of data gathering is more restricted in focus than the first. It concerns just one or two major aspects of school life. Data gathering at this level may involve the whole faculty, but more commonly it involves a subgroup of teachers who are particularly concerned with the issue. Often this level of data gathering is precipitated by an initial problem statement.
- The third level of data gathering is more restricted still and is normally located at the level of classroom teaching. The detailed data on classroom teaching and learning are not generally of interest to the whole faculty, or even to large groups of teachers. Data on classroom behavior are useful to the teacher concerned with self-reflection and development, of interest to an observer, and of interest to an administrator who may have teacher appraisal responsibilities. But, as this information is not shared in any detail among the faculty as a whole, strictly speaking it does not fall within Phase 1 of the School Development process. It becomes more important at Phases 3 and 4.

Data Gathering at the School Level

The four approaches to data gathering at the whole-of-school level are the following:

- a formal review initiated and performed by the school itself;
- an "illuminative" evaluation on the occasion of a new principal arriving at a school;
- the use of a consultant from outside the school;
- the use of an instrument to measure some global indicator of effectiveness such as school climate, school health, school culture, or leadership.

The first three of these approaches will involve the faculty in a considerable outlay of time and energy, but should form the foundation for an effective process of School Development. The final approach is more superficial, and may or may not serve the purpose of getting teachers to reflect seriously on their practices and values.

School Review

The school review is one of the most thorough approaches available for gathering data and generating organizational self-reflection. The term "school review" suggests a number of options, but it is possible to identify some elements common to most:

- reviews are intensive phases of data gathering and feedback lasting from a few days to several weeks;
- reviews tend to involve all or most of the faculty in gathering and discussing data;
- reviews may involve representatives from the district, parents, the local community, the students, and neighboring educational institutions;

- virtually all reviews will examine the curriculum and instructional programs by attempting to clarify goals and objectives and by assessing the effectiveness of the school's teaching and learning programs;
- some reviews will adopt a broader perspective and examine features such as community expectations, teacher morale, or financial and general resource management; others may focus more narrowly on the legal and mandatory obligations of the school;
- the findings of reviews are generally made known to the local school community and form the basis for a school's later developmental efforts.

Observers of reviews in the past have noted a number of shortcomings in the process. Some principals have not understood the central role they needed to play in the guidance and direction of the review; many teachers have not had the technical or interpersonal skills needed to collect and analyze the data; and many schools have not known what to do with the data when collected (Robinson 1982).

These are serious but not insurmountable difficulties. There remains an important place for whole-of-school reviews. With more guidance about the process that should be followed, such reviews could lead to a worthwhile process of School Development. They provide a school's faculty and community with the opportunity to take stock and to ask the following important questions:

- As a school community, what are we trying to do?
- Can we list what we are achieving?
- What evidence do we have?
- What do we as teachers, and as a school, do well?

- What do we do badly, or fail to do, and why?
- What prevents us from providing an education that is appropriate for every student?
- How can we make the best use of our resources and improve the quality of teaching and learning?

The review process is not a simple, straightforward one. Clem Adelman and Robin Alexander (1982) have documented the problems and the processes that any institution is likely to encounter when it engages in a process of self-evaluation. Most of the literature on institutional evaluation relates to studies performed by outside consultants and is principally concerned with questions of technique and method. Adelman and Alexander, on the other hand, write about their association with two colleges which, over the course of several years, attempted to evaluate themselves. Their work is particularly relevant to this discussion of School Development because many of the values and assumptions underlying those two evaluation projects closely resemble those already discussed in this book. The institutions they were evaluating espoused values of democracy, pluralism, and mutual accountability. Accordingly, the model of evaluation they adopted reflected this concern for democratic values, with heavy emphasis on data gathering by participants, extensive analysis and discussion of data by the members of the organization, and a broad negotiation of the implications of all data. But while the public rhetoric of the institutions may have emphasized democracy, pluralism, and participation, in practice there was a recurring tendency to suppress dissent, to exert pressure toward consensus, and to take action on the basis of minority decisions. Adelman and Alexander make the critical observation that the challenges in institutional self-evaluations are "interpersonal, political and organizational, rather than methodological" (1982, 1).

An Illuminative Evaluation

School reviews provide opportunities for a school to collect data about a wide range of school operations. A change of principal provides another opportunity. Any new principal should engage in a period of data gathering and reflection during the first few months of arriving at a new school. Usually this is an informal, personal process of observing and learning. The rest of the school continues in its normal routine while the new incumbent tries to come to grips with the assignment. There are two ways that this period of data gathering and reflection could be made more effective, both for the principal and for the school:

- *systematic data gathering*—it should be possible to anticipate the kind of information that will be needed even before arriving at the school, and to devise procedures and even instruments to help gather this data.
- *involving teachers in reviewing the major features of the school operation for their own benefit as well*—for instance, if the principal wants to find out about the procedures for reporting student progress within the school, it is much more profitable to engage a group of faculty in the task of gathering information and debating the present system than to let the principal form conclusions from isolated observations in a context not yet entirely familiar.

This kind of investigation has many of the attributes of an evaluation, but a particular kind of evaluation. Malcolm Parlett and David Hamilton (1977) coined the term "illuminative evaluation" to describe an approach that was more concerned with description and interpretation than with measurement and prediction. Whereas conventional approaches to evaluation attempt to study instructional approaches (such as learning using technology, a new curriculum, or a schedul-

An illuminative evaluation is therefore an ecological exercise–an attempt to describe and understand all the major networks of cultural, social, institutional, and psychological variables, and the way they influence one another.

ing framework) as discrete formal entities with specified objectives, procedures, and outcomes, illuminative evaluation claims that such learning systems can only be studied and understood within the context of the "learning milieu."

An illuminative evaluation is therefore an ecological exercise–an attempt to describe and understand all the major networks of cultural, social, institutional, and psychological variables, and the way they influence one another. Such a broad-based approach to evaluation requires a flexible and eclectic approach to data gathering. The methods of gathering data will be influenced largely by the nature of the problem, instructional program, or institution that is being investigated, but the overall study is likely to have three stages for a newly appointed elementary or middle school principal. These stages can initiate the first two steps of School Development.

- First, the principal's task is to become familiar with the day-to-day activities of the school and the main features of the school's existing policy. For example, if there was an issue about homework the exploratory stage would lead to the identification of things such as the variation in teachers' expectations about the amount of time students spend on homework that could warrant closer study.
- Second, as these problematic aspects are identified, the evaluation moves into a second stage of more focused, directed data gathering, in this case a survey of teachers' current expectations by grade level. While the focus is on homework, the data will reveal information about other important instructional themes—the extent to which homework is based on classroom teaching and learning, teachers' understandings of how learning is reinforced through practice, how much responsibility is given to students for their own learning, the extent to which good work and study habits are

being developed, and even the extent to which parents are involved in supporting classroom learning–that offer insights into the way the school is functioning.
- Third, the principal and the members of the faculty seek to explain and interpret the information they have gathered.

When following the illuminative evaluation approach, the data analysis stage is not an activity that must await the collection of all the data. Teachers should be involved in a constant cycle of requestioning and refining as they gather data on their selected themes. In the homework example, new lines of inquiry such as what contribution parents could make to the development of a consistent homework policy as might be proposed from an analysis of the survey results could be explored immediately. Other lines of inquiry that seem to be resolving themselves can be abandoned quickly, rather than impede the process. In spite of this interplay of data gathering and analysis, there is a need to continually collect and report findings to the faculty. It is on the basis of this reporting, the faculty's reaction to it, and further analysis, that the school can continue into a further phase of the School Development process.

The Outside Consultant

Although this chapter has been addressing the question of how a school might collect data about its operations, it is not always possible to separate this from a consideration of who should do the collecting. We have suggested that it is very important that teachers should be involved in data gathering, and that such involvement seems to be almost a necessary prerequisite to effective School Development. While this remains true, there are very definite advantages to using someone from outside the school community to get this process of data gathering and feedback

There are very definite advantages to using someone from outside the school community to get this process of data gathering and feedback started.

started. An example of data gathering by external consultants may illustrate the contribution an outsider can make to initiating a School Development process.

In an earlier publication, Tom Prebble and David Stewart described an intervention at Belmont School (1981, 17–30). The principal and faculty had embarked on a series of discussions aimed originally at improving the morale and general level of functioning of the school. These discussions had led to the construction of a "plan of action" that proposed a number of measures aimed at the more specific challenges of improving the relationship between the school and the community and providing more assistance for students requiring additional support. Aware that the proposal did not match the initial concerns, and worried that the initial momentum and enthusiasm of the faculty discussions could be lost, the principal invited the two researchers to act as consultants.

The first step was to gather data about the "plan of action," about the processes by which it had been arrived at, and about the problems and challenges for which the plan had seemed to be an answer. This was undertaken in two ways. First, a selection was made from teachers who were willing to be involved to ensure that all sections of the school were represented. About half the faculty became directly involved this way and were interviewed following a set of guidelines. To avoid disrupting classroom work, the consultants took it in turns to interview the teachers. As one consultant interviewed a teacher outside the classroom, the other consultant would take over the class for the fifteen to twenty minutes needed. Additionally, the members of each specialist group were asked to discuss a series of issues at their next meeting and to record their reactions, which could be analyzed by the consultants. The input from these two sources of data, plus a series of discussions with the principal, formed the basis for the feedback from the consultants to the faculty. The important point about using outside consultants in this case is that the consultants themselves are, in one important sense at least, not the change agents. Since they are unable to make the changes within the school, the real decision, in the final analysis, lies with the principal. In this example the data gathered by the consultants and the collaborative analysis of the data by the faculty were what finally lead to a particular decision being made.

Standard Instruments

The approaches to data gathering all make the assumption that each school has its own unique problems. This implies a further assumption that schools are generally best advised to devise their own means of gathering data on their problems.

Once a problem or concern has been identified the following questions could form a useful guide to data gathering:

- What is the issue and how would we usually address it?
- What can we infer, therefore, about our school culture?
- How did we get to be this way?
- What is the range of options open to us?

Schools not wishing to invest the considerable amount of time and energy required to devise their own data-gathering instruments, or for those looking for a few guidelines in this kind of data gathering, there are a number of standardized instruments available. Many of these instruments have been tested for reliability and validity, standardized for different types of organizations, and form the basis of a number of research studies. This kind of refinement and stan-

Climate is concerned with the process and style of the school's organizational life rather than its content and substance (Sergiovanni 1991, 218).

dardization is vital if it is intended to make comparisons among institutions. If the sole purpose is to enable the members of an organization to collect useful information about their own institution, then the choice of instruments can be less rigorous. Schools always have the option to seek assistance in constructing their own questionnaires.

Data can be gathered about a number of dimensions. In general, social scientists have concentrated their attention on a number of constructs assumed to be directly related to overall organizational effectiveness. The more prominent of these are organizational climate and culture. It may be helpful to understand how these constructs have been measured.

School Climate

While the notion of school climate seems to be a useful way for members of an organization to conceptualize a number of important, if subtle, processes, it is an extremely difficult construct to define. If pressed for a definition, people are likely to turn to other analogies such as "atmosphere," "tone," or even "personality." Social scientists attempting to measure this elusive property have generally described climate as a perceptual phenomenon, defining climate as the internal quality of the organization as experienced by its members (Hoy and Miskel 1982, 185). Another writer suggests that climate is concerned with the process and style of the school's organizational life rather than its content and substance (Sergiovanni 1991, 218).

These definitions narrow the field to the perceptions of organizational members, and mean that we can validly assess the climate of a school by asking its members how they feel about the life of the institution. But what questions are asked, and which members are asked them? The research tradition that has been most influential in the study of school climate was initiated by Andrew Halpin and Donald Croft in the early 1960s. They deliberately restricted their attention to determinants of climate that they considered to be the most potent influence–that is, the impact of the behavior of teachers and the principal on school climate. Other determinants such as the organizational structure, the environment of the school, or the students were ignored. The instrument they devised–the Organization Climate Description Questionnaire (Halpin 1966)–consists of 64 items. Half of the items are intended to measure aspects of the principal's behavior, and these are divided into four subtests: aloofness, production emphasis, thrust, and consideration. The other 32 items are intended to measure dimensions of teacher behavior, namely disengagement, hindrance, esprit, and intimacy. There have been numerous attempts to improve on this instrument. For example, the New Zealand Council for Educational Research (NZCER) has published the School Level Environment Questionnaire (SLEQ) (1990).

The New Zealand instrument is limited by the fact that only teachers are asked to complete it, and their subjective impressions rather than other perhaps more objective data are being sought. Also, the focus of the questions is restricted to the behavior of the principal and other staff members. Nevertheless a number of schools have found the document and the process useful in moving toward a more collaborative culture in the school.

School Culture

A particular school's culture can be defined as "the way we do things in this school, and why we think we are doing them that way"–the habitual patterns of beliefs, attitudes, values, and activities shared and engaged in by members of

School Development could be understood as the process by which a school comes to align its culture and structures more isomorphically with the mission or goals and objectives of the institution.

an organization. School Development could be understood as the process by which a school comes to align its culture and structures more isomorphically with the mission or goals and objectives of the institution. Charles Handy's distinctions among "role," "task," "power," and "person" cultures seem to offer a useful basis for the analysis of school culture (Handy 1978, 1990). Handy's short questionnaire is designed to start organizational members thinking about the types of culture that predominate in their organizations. The questionnaire is comprised of a set of statements about the values, beliefs, and behaviors that might characterize an organization. These are organized under nine headings, from statements about the qualities of a good boss to statements about the function of competition within the organization. There are four contrasting statements under each heading, and respondents are asked to rank them in order of which best describes the organization in which they work. Having completed this exercise, respondents then consider all the statements again and rerank them in terms of their own preference for how the organization should be managed. The complete questionnaire can be found in Handy's earlier publication, *Gods of Management* (1978, 83–88).

As with the Organization Climate Description Questionnaire and other climate questionnaires, a number of qualifications must be made concerning this instrument. The responses of different teachers will vary, Handy suggests, often as a function of their position in the hierarchy.

Thomas Sergiovanni offers another interpretation of school culture. He explains the concept as a metaphor that "helps direct attention to the symbols, behavioral regularities, ceremonies, and even myths that communicate to people the underlying value and beliefs that are shared by the members of the organization" (1991, 218).

His use of levels of culture, artifacts, perspectives, values, and assumptions provides a useful means of gathering data and then constructing a school culture profile during School Development Phase 1 and Phase 2 activities. As a further caveat, it is important to recognize that although there are clear benefits for schools from having a strong and identified culture, strong cultures can also militate against change.

Data Gathering on Specific Issues Within the School

The previous section has discussed how a school community might gather data of a general nature about its operations and how the analysis and discussion of these data might initiate a process of School Development. This kind of whole-of-faculty exercise may be a very exciting and totally necessary way to gain the initial commitment of a school faculty. It is unlikely, however, that the whole of the faculty will continue to be involved in data gathering on a continual basis, or that the focus will remain for long at the school-wide level. Data gathering will remain a central feature of the School Development effort but it is likely to involve only a selection of the school community at any one time, and focus on specific issues.

The challenge for those leading this phase of the School Development process is to develop the habit of data gathering as an almost automatic response within the faculty. When a problem is raised during faculty discussions, the first response should not be "what is the solution?" but "what information do we have about this problem?" Collaborative problem solving can only work if it is based on shared perceptions of the dimensions of the problem. The best way to ensure that teachers agree about the nature of the prob-

There is no one way of gathering data. A lot depends on the nature of the issue or problem.

lem is to engage in systematic data gathering and feedback prior to considering action alternatives. There is no one way of gathering data. A lot depends on the nature of the issue or problem.

Take this first example from Lakeview Elementary School, and the issue of instructional resources. Lakeview faculty had decided to abandon the basal reader as a core reading resource and instead base instructional reading around literature series and trade books. The issue was how to ensure there was a sufficient range of instructional materials suited to the new approach. Traditionally, the faculty only had access to material that was already in classroom collections. Over the years these collections had been supplemented from purchases teachers made from their annual allocation of funds and their own private collections. Was there a more effective way of utilizing this considerable resource? Indeed, was there any way of knowing the quality and extent of it? The faculty debated the advantages and disadvantages of a centrally shared collection. At first there was some enthusiasm. This began to evaporate as problems started to multiply. What about the books that are traditionally only available to certain grade levels? What if special collections are not available when they are needed? Who would be responsible for managing the new arrangement? Where would it be housed? How would it be organized? Sensing resistance, yet seeing the proposal as a way to begin faculty collaboration about improving teaching and learning in reading and writing through a more balanced program, the principal saw the opportunity to take an initiative. She suggested an inventory of the existing classroom collections to see what was available and whether they would be worth considering as a central collection. She had the faculty agree only to the collection of data. A form was prepared that sought the title, number, and purchase or publication date of each resource, including books and other media. Also requested was a judgment about the appropriate use for each resource and an opinion about its quality. Teachers were requested to include community purchased resources, but not personal material.

The analysis of the data was revealing. The existing classroom collections varied considerably in range, suitability for a balanced program, and quality as literature. The data itself carried a clear message. Of course, not all the faculty agreed that a centralized collection was the most appropriate option. Some wanted more funding to add to their existing classroom collections. In the end, the quality and economic arguments won out, along with a report to the faculty from a small faculty team about how some of the questions that had been raised could be addressed. The comparative data gathered about upgrading the range and quality of existing materials, particularly for kindergarten through second grade, against the cost of providing sufficient funds for each classroom to meet the new program initiative, were compelling. The faculty agreed to trial a shared central resource collection beginning in the first year with kindergarten through second grade. Following a review on a specified date toward the end of the school year, a decision would be made whether or not to extend the collection further up the grades.

The second example may appear at first glance to affect only the fifth-grade teachers of Elm Street School. It is surprising how an analysis of the data collected by this group impacted down to kindergarten. A question was raised about the kinds of information being sent by fifth-grade teachers at Elm Street to the local middle school. It appeared that Elm Street teachers sent what each thought would be relevant to the middle school teachers. Some forwarded only the final report card with letter grades. Some offered detailed analyses of current running records and copies of student work in writing and spelling, mathematical processing, and broader life skills. Others provided narrative statements of a more general kind in addition to current test results. There was little consistency and no clear expectations about what was relevant or appropriate information.

The principals of Elm Street, other district elementary schools, and the principal of the middle school agreed that more consistent, quality information should be available. All faculties agreed to consider the issue. Following separate discussions and a further meeting of the principals with faculty representatives, it was decided that two groups of data would be collected. The fifth-grade teachers would collect data about what information they currently forwarded to the middle school. The sixth-grade teachers would indicate what current information was useful and what additional information would also be relevant. The information was to be collected by simple questionnaires and followed up with a joint meeting between the district's fifth- and sixth-grade teachers. At this meeting small groups of teachers from the elementary schools would interview a sixth-grade teacher, then together report their findings. The detailed results of the survey analysis and discussions need not concern us here, other than to note that a new portfolio of information was agreed to. The consequence of this data collection and the subsequent action, however, provides an interesting postscript. At Elm Street School the fifth-grade teachers began to question the quality of information they received at the beginning of the school year from the fourth-grade teachers, raising the whole issue of time lost getting to know students, and how the quality of information being given to teachers in the next grade year could be improved. In the end, this discussion not only involved all of the other grades including kindergarten, but raised the whole question of what was expected as learning outcomes at each grade level. But that's another story.

These case studies also illustrate that data gathering need not be a separate, complex, time-consuming activity. Both cases are illustrations of important staff developmental opportunities. In the first case, the decision to develop an instructional resource center could have a profound impact on the teaching of reading as teachers became more familiar with the resources they put together to support various reading approaches (certainly what the principal hoped would happen) and made further purchase decisions. In the second case, the methods adopted for data gathering gave real purpose to a professional dialogue between elementary and middle school faculties. What is more, it was an opportunity for teachers to see that the quality of the information that they provide determines the quality of information that is available for later decisions. Looking again at the examples, it can be noted that the following techniques were used:

- questionnaires to elicit facts;
- questionnaires to elicit opinions;
- interviews;
- group discussions.

Depending on the circumstances and the information sought, data can also be gathered using:

- simulations and case studies to initiate discussion;
- documentary sources;
- direct observation.

This is by no means an exhaustive list, but it illustrates the range of possibilities for schools at-

Data gathering need not be a separate, complex, time-consuming activity.

Cooperative and collaborative group structures are influential in increasing both positive attitudes toward one another and the likelihood that concern and thoughtful attention will be given to each other's points of view.

tempting to gather data about their work processes.

Phase 2. Collaborative Analysis

Data gathering is a first step–an important first step, but no more than that. If members of a school community have invested effort in gathering data on an agreed problem or challenge, then they will want to discuss the results of their efforts. They may decide that the data do not always match their initial beliefs or assumptions and they are likely to have discussed that. They will vary among themselves as to the interpretation of the data and the values they bring to that interpretation. In a typical school with a mix of attitudes and understandings among the faculty they may uncover as much disagreement and conflict in the data as they do consensus and harmony. This raises two issues:

- Why it is important to establish collaboration within a School Development framework?
- What sort of training and development might support a faculty learning to become more collaborative?

Why Collaborate?

There is an impressive list of research supporting the claim that cooperative and collaborative group structures are influential in increasing both positive attitudes toward one another and the likelihood that concern and thoughtful attention will be given to each other's points of view. The same data support the likelihood that concern and thoughtful attention will be given to individual viewpoints and original ideas (Kraus 1980, 96; Johnson et al. 1988). When making decisions within schools there is seldom just one possible solution. A collaborative approach enables groups of professionals to delay the final decision for a time while a wide range of options is presented and divergent thinking is welcomed. Information sharing and feedback have already been established in School Development Phase 1. A collaborative stance further encourages questioning the value of such information and the relative priority that should be given to the problems that it highlights. The involvement of everyone in the process of addressing a problem does not, in any way, force them to agree to a particular solution. What can happen is that all become committed to test the workability of a particular outcome for a specific time. This concept of collaboration leading to action is an important one. It is not enough to agree to discuss a problem. There must always be the assumption of action to follow. Organizations may need to develop clear and precise mechanisms for ensuring that this happens. In summary, collaboration:

- allows individuals to become genuinely more effective;
- provides incentives, support, and encouragement for individual initiatives;
- gains access to the variety of thinking and activity embedded in colleagues' repertoires;
- makes creative use of the conflict of legitimate individual differences;
- perceives such difference as variety rather than as competition;
- maximizes the energy of faculty members toward more effective teaching and learning.

Any plan for increasing faculty collaboration would need to include the following:

- agreement regarding times and procedures for collaborative endeavor;
- an array of effective decision-making methods;

- sound strategies for resolving conflict;
- procedures for an easy flow of communications among teachers;
- the setting of realistic goals;
- an agreement to persist with a collaborative effort;
- an understanding that not all problems are amenable to group solutions;
- an agreement to refine and practice the skills necessary to promote efficient group processes.

Participation in group discussion implies that an individual learns both from hearing the ideas of others and from seeing the reaction of colleagues to their own contributions. The growth of the group depends on these inputs being integrated with the individual's own thoughts. Consequently it becomes very important that procedures that allow perception checks to be made are an integral part of the group's functioning. Alvin Zander (1982, 31) suggests that a group discussion serves five purposes by:

- helping members recognize what they do not know but should;
- providing occasions for members to get answers to questions;
- letting members get advice on matters that bother them;
- letting persons share ideas and derive a common wisdom;
- allowing members to learn about one another as persons.

Furthermore, the group will be more productive and members will get a greater degree of satisfaction from their efforts if they clearly know the purpose of their deliberations, the goals they hope to achieve, and the methods that will be used in any particular instance.

Having established a case for collaboration within a school development framework it is necessary for the principal to work with teachers to develop the appropriate skills of teamwork and communication. There is training literature available for skills and interpersonal relation- ships, together with a range of suggestions pre- sented in Appendix A.

Increasing the Level of Collaboration

Once the members of a school community have gathered data about a problem or challenge, they will want to talk about this information. If it is a controversial issue, they will bring strong convictions and personal attitudes to these ex- changes. It cannot be taken for granted that these discussions will lead to harmony and agree- ment. In fact, if due attention is not paid to group processes at this point, there is every likelihood that any disagreement among faculty will be deepened through discussion rather than re- solved by it. It is important for the school commu- nity to pay explicit attention to its group processes at this point to make sure that this col- lective reflection and analysis is productive and positive, rather than acrimonious or divisive.

Many groups find it helpful to undergo some training or coaching in the processes of group communication as they begin to commit to a more intensive process of collaboration. This coaching need not be complex or technical. Again, refer to Appendix A, where there is a selection of group process training techniques that are just some of the many hundreds available. It is suggested that a faculty appoint a process facilitator to guide this aspect of their School Development work. This person would not need to be a specialist in group processes, though this would be helpful. The school counselor or some other faculty mem- ber with training in group processes could be well suited to this work. The skills they use every day to help students interact more productively can also be used with their colleagues. This facilitator would agree to stay out of the discussion of the subject at hand, concentrating instead on the group processes being used or trialled by colleagues, and intervening from time to time to comment on group processes being used or suggesting a new technique to try.

A desire to increase the quantity and quality of collaborative work in a school is a very good beginning. However, in most situations it will be necessary to increase the level of interactive skills that teachers use when working with each other. The examples in Appendix A have been treated as discrete categories of group process skills. In reality, skills and procedures will often cross boundaries. The Professional Development Consultation cycle discussed in more detail in the next section often effectively prevents conflict and encourages teachers to have a series of regular, systematic conferences with the principal to develop their own job in a satisfying manner. The point of including the various interpersonal and intergroup examples is to assist schools that seek to increase their level of faculty participation and collaboration. They will also serve as a checklist against which schools can review their faculty relationships, and as a guide for their plans to improve these relationships.

Phase 3. Structural Change

A large proportion of the research literature on educational innovation is devoted to studying changes in the organization and structure of schools rather than to the more fundamental educational issues of curriculum, pedagogy, and evaluation. Structural changes tend to be more visible and more dramatic than changes in the mode or content of classroom teaching. They involve more people than do classroom innovations, and they tend to be more hotly contested both within the institution and in the wider community.

At the system level there are the seesawing debates over half-day or full-day kindergarten, the place of preschools and middle schools, and the optimum age to transfer from the elementary school. There are debates about time engaged in learning, the "long block" in the intermediate grades, how to provide for special learning needs through "push-in" rather than "pull-out" programs, and arrangements for bilingual programs. As educational fashions change we observe trends toward multi-age or non-graded classrooms and the existing structures for dealing with classroom behavior problems and the disabled competing with policies supporting inclusion for students who would otherwise be in special facilities. Within schools a wide range of organizational structures are set up to address the social and custodial needs of students such as counseling networks, before- and after-school programs, and homework support. Both schools and community agencies, usually conjointly, have developed these structures. Supports for the curriculum and the teaching and learning programs offer plenty of scope for structural innovations such as shared classrooms, open area instruction, faculty or grade grouping, family grouping, six-day timetables, tracking, learning contracts, expanded options, and so on. The list is endless.

It is very easy for school administrators to become preoccupied with the challenge of implementing a structural innovation within their schools, and forget that such changes are simply organizational means to an educational or social end. It is also easy to forget that structures are like guidelines for the behavior of organizational members, and if these structures are ignored, it is unlikely that new structural arrangements will be any more effective. It is important that the structural change phase should take its proper place in a School Development sequence. Phase 1

It is very easy for school administrators to become preoccupied with the challenge of implementing a structural innovation within their schools, and forget that such changes are simply organizational means to an educational or social end.

of the process of School Development serves to heighten the perceptions of the school community to the way the school operates. As the faculty debate their varying perceptions, they move into more collaborative working relationships and begin to see the school as a shared collective endeavor, rather than as the locus for their own uncontested, autonomous action. Through Phase 2 the faculty are likely to realize that existing structural arrangements no longer facilitate these new working relationships and understandings. A consensus may emerge about the new structural arrangements that will be needed as the process moves into Phase 3. The test of these new structures will be how quickly and effectively teachers are able to use them to focus on the fundamental issues of the curriculum, teaching, and learning, which become the key focus for Phase 4. There is no shortage of structural options for the modern school, but unless the faculty base their selection on a very thorough analysis of their existing issues, problems, challenges, and aspirations, it is highly unlikely that a new structure will serve them any better than did a previous one. Again, if it seems to be stating the obvious about making a case for a considered, sequential approach to structural change, there are any number of examples of unsuccessful restructuring because the proposed approach to change was neither considered nor sequential.

Process Rather Than Product

In the discussions of Phases 1 and 2 of the School Development process, it was possible to abstract a number of general principles and discuss a variety of techniques that might apply to any school. For instance, various instruments for gathering data about school climate or culture were described, and a number of techniques for improving the level of interpersonal interaction within a faculty were offered. When considering structural and program change, it is not possible to offer solutions that can be applied in all situations. School Development is concerned with a process rather than a product. The objective is to assist schools to work out solutions to their own problems and challenges and not to impose someone else's solutions on them. It may be more useful to describe how a number of schools have used a School Development sequence to arrive at their own structural and program innovations rather than to suggest that the solutions these schools arrived at have any intrinsic merit and apply in other contexts.

Earlier in the chapter we described a new principal's efforts to gather data about policy and practice for homework. The data gathered confirmed that teachers even at the same grade level had quite different expectations about the assignment of homework. The issue had come up because a parent with siblings at different grade levels saw different standards being applied by teachers and brought the matter to the attention of the new principal. The faculty collected the data in one of the ways set out as part of Phase 1 of the School Development process. During Phase 2 of the process a number of teachers discussed the results of their data gathering–how other schools assigned homework, their own previous experience, through conversations with colleagues, what the district expected, and just as importantly, the expectations of parents. During Phase 3, the principal and teachers began procedures for a standard, school-wide approach to setting homework. One of the key structural innovations they considered was a homework center, established for children on later buses, those awaiting parents, and those who arrived early at school. Another solution was to schedule a homework reminder time a few minutes before dismissal to ensure that students understood their homework obligations. Parents were involved at

How many schools jump spasmodically from one structural innovation to the next, never taking the time to discover whether they fully understood or needed the innovations in the first place?

all three phases of this program. This resulted in developing a consistent homework policy with its attendant structural supports, which in turn gave parents, as well as the faculty, a stake in the success of the innovation.

Why is it necessary to delay introducing structural change until the teachers and the school community have moved through the first two phases of the School Development sequence? Why are these first two phases of data gathering and collaborative reflection so important? The following brief case study may help to clarify.

It is a Great Solution, But What Was the Problem?

Tom Prebble, one of the authors, spent a year observing a school undergoing a radical structural change that took place without any prior consensus being reached about the objectives of that change (Prebble 1978; Prebble and Stewart 1981, 65). A western Canadian high school moved to a four-day instructional week, compressing the 1,400 minutes of weekly class contact into four teaching days instead of the usual five. Individuals and groups on the faculty, in the community, and in the school district administration held some strong opinions concerning the objectives and payoffs of the new timetable. In the beginning, most people supported the new arrangement, but for varying and often mutually incompatible reasons. It took some people months, even years, to discover that their own perceptions of the purpose of the four-day week were not shared by their colleagues. The four-day timetable endured for several years, resisting the efforts of several teams of evaluators to assess how effective it had been in influencing curriculum, teaching, or student achievement.

This is not an isolated example. How many schools jump spasmodically from one structural innovation to the next, never taking the time to discover whether they fully understood or needed the innovations in the first place, and never gaining the full educational benefits from each arrangement before opting for its successor?

Structural change should always be a consequence of shared data gathering and shared innovation rather than a catch-all solution to a range of vaguely defined and perceived problems. An illustration at a comparatively simple level could occur as a school faculty considers the matter of supervision of out-of-class time. Say it was reported to the school administration that student behavioral problems were occurring with certain groups of students at recess. The tendency is for the school to move immediately to a school-wide implementation of new supervision procedures. A School Development approach would turn instead to the gathering of some appropriate data, seeking information about the following:

- Where were the problems occurring?
- How many students were involved?
- How often did this occur?
- What about areas of the playground where there were no problems?
- What makes the difference in these problem-free areas?

If the teachers who were most concerned with the problem were able to be given time to gather this kind of information, then so much the better. If most of the faculty were able to rapidly report back their perceptions and observations, perhaps by monitoring observed behavior in a systematic way for a day or two, then a wide variety of relevant data would be available for review.

The next step would be to discuss the data and perhaps trial some of the ideas for a short time to gauge their relative effectiveness. The third stage would be consideration of policy that

confirmed the most reliable and effective measures. This would be the structural change.

Phase 4. A Focus on Teaching and Learning

People interested in promoting changes in
curriculum, teaching, and learning programs in
schools frequently have difficulty accepting that
such change efforts may need to be delayed until
the school has made some progress with the first
three phases in the School Development process.
Yet, the need to develop the curriculum and improve classroom practice is inevitably seen as urgent. Usually, the feeling is that a school cannot
afford to wait for a period of months, or even for a
year or two, before embarking on intensive interventions at the level of classroom practice. However, a number of studies have established that
for an innovation in teaching practice to be fully
effective, teachers must be convinced that it
meets an important need, and that it will be an
improvement over existing practice. This is the
contribution of the first, or data gathering, phase.
Teachers must also experience the active conceptual synthesis of their colleagues and be given opportunities to renegotiate their involvement in
the innovation as the need arises. This is the cooperation that arises from collaboration in Phase
2. Finally, the school must commit its resources
and structures to supporting the innovation so
that there are as few obstacles in the path of the
innovation as possible. This is the contribution of
Phase 3. Only when these challenges have been
resolved, or teachers have the appropriate strategies to deal with them, can the full resources of
energy be directed to improving classroom practice.

Following the School Development sequence
of Quadrant 1 in this manner allows all the en-

ergy in the school to be applied to the main function of the school—improving the quality of teaching and learning. In many schools teachers are distracted from this focus by factors they perceive to be outside their control. A simple example might be the manner in which students' arguments and disagreements from recess extend into the sessions that follow these breaks. Classroom teachers, often with some justification, attribute these problems to the quality of playground supervision, while at the same time having to adjust their intentions and approaches to cope with the consequential disruption. Restoring an appropriate learning environment soaks up energy that could otherwise have been applied to engagement on learning tasks—the real business of the classroom. Using the four phases of the School Development process works toward the resolution of this kind of issue. There are further examples of the power of the School Development process in action offered through a number of case studies explored in the next chapter.

Chapter 5

The Power of the School Development Process

In Part III we will examine Quadrant II of School Development, the process of individual development. It is useful to consider the power of the process of data gathering and collaborative analysis to build capacity within a school community before leaving a discussion of the four phases of School Development in Quadrant I.

A key purpose of the school is to meet the diverse range of learning needs of its students. As well as meeting student needs, the building of capacity through the School Development process is also meeting the learning needs of the faculty, parents, administrators, and the principal. We have selected a number of significant dimensions–there will be many more–by which a school community can continue to add value to the work it does by utilizing School Development. We have included case studies to help illustrate some of these dimensions.

An Improved Knowledge Base Within the Organization

A fundamental tenet of School Development is that collaborative leadership can only operate

Collaborative leadership can only operate on the basis of ready access to high-quality data.

on the basis of ready access to high-quality data. The faculty that has a good working knowledge of the major organizational and instructional programs operating within the school has also developed the habit of data gathering. Schools operating in this way are more likely to resolve organizational problems since the basis upon which decision making is founded is reliable data collected and shared with teachers and the administration.

Greater Clarity Over How the School Is Working

A faculty wishing to work more collaboratively and effectively will be developing a shared view of how the school is working. Teachers will be called upon to give more attention to the school's instructional goals, the objectives they will pursue individually in their classrooms and within their grade level groups, and how these objectives are translated into consistent, effective, school-wide policies and instructional programs. Much of the important work on school cultures will take place in Phase 2. The challenge at this point is for members of the school to come to understand the differing points of view of other members of the organization, and to learn to work collaboratively, rather than in isolation, in the negotiation and pursuit of their collective instructional goals.

As a faculty begins to make progress with these discussions, it is likely that members will find that the existing decision-making structures are inadequate–an example is the open faculty meeting–for the purpose of revising curriculum and developing new action plans. At this stage some restructuring of the traditional ways of doing things may be necessary. The faculty may wish to consider working first in grade level meetings on a common topic of goal clarification before reporting back to the whole faculty, or alternatively, assign to a particular group the responsibility for a draft report on a goal issue to be reported at a later faculty meeting. There are any number of ways that faculties can reshape the way decisions can be reached. The most important aspect is that the faculty works together and sees the development of new decision-making structures as an integral part of the School Development process. The following is a case in point.

The faculty at Second Street School had been working for some months on its broad goals for reading and writing. Through the early phase of its School Development initiative the idea that faculty meeting time become an opportunity for professional discussion was greeted with more relief than enthusiasm by teachers who, up to that point, spent almost an hour each week endlessly debating the student behavioral problems arising at recess, dismissal, and on the buses. Yet, even the faculty meetings focusing on reading and writing had fallen into a familiar pattern. The same people had plenty to say, the same strong opinions tended to dominate, and semantic games offered little hint of even broad consensus upon which a decision could be reached. Despite good intentions, goal statements did not come easily to the faculty at Second Street. There was a possibility, the principal suggested, that the discussion might be addressing the wrong question, and that they should be asking themselves "What is it as a school we really *value* in a reader and a writer?" The principal suggested that the faculty not discuss the question first as a whole faculty, but consider it in grade level groups over the following two weeks, then report their discussions on chart paper to be displayed at the next whole faculty meeting. The most surprising outcome was the degree of unanimity in the statements and the changed tone of the ensuing full

The way to achieve this change of direction is to provide members with more opportunities to work together and more skills for working collaboratively.

faculty discussion. Second Street was now further on its way to developing its goals for literacy teaching and learning, having experienced that the *process* of collaboration itself suggested a different sort of *structure* for working together.

Increased Participation of Teachers in Executive Decision Making

Collaboration is a reciprocal process. If the school's leadership is looking for a greater commitment to shared goals and objectives, then the school community must be allowed full participation in the important decisions concerning those policies and practices. Learning to participate, for the most part, is a process that begins in Phase 2. The aim of this phase is to encourage the faculty and students to think about their school as "our school" rather than "my school" or "the principal's school." It is a phase where the concept of mutual responsibility begins to emerge.

The way to achieve this change of direction is to provide members with more opportunities to work together and more skills for working collaboratively. As already noted, some of the skills and values that will facilitate this process are offered in Appendix A. Processes of group interaction and deliberation can be improved by training in these kinds of skills, and there is considerable improvement in the quality of interaction among a faculty that has as much concern for the process of reaching a decision as it does for the quality of the decision itself.

In Chapter 4, the decision Lakeview School took to establish a reading instructional resource collection was discussed. The Lakeview faculty soon learned upon embarking on the School Development process that the mission the school had established for itself was not something decoratively framed in the hallway or lost in a bottom drawer. The principal actively encouraged faculty participation in key decisions by encouraging the collection of data and collaborative discussion leading the faculty to comfortably agree that "we" have made the decision. With the school's mission clearly in mind (it emphasized excellence and equity) she would ask the faculty about each proposal, "Whose interests would be served by a favorable decision?" (equity) and, "Would such a decision directly support improving student achievement?" (excellence). It got to the point where members began asking the questions themselves before raising an idea with the principal. Decisions about the school schedule, for example, using the criteria of the mission statement, had to clearly have the students' interests at heart, not just those of the organization or its teachers. At Lakeview, mutual responsibility began with the principal continually reminding teachers of what they had *already agreed to* as the school's mission.

Improved Systems for the Supervision of Work

One of the most important and challenging tasks of educational leadership is supervision—making sure that the members of the faculty are doing their job effectively, while at the same time supporting them to do it better. School leadership, now more than ever, poses the challenge of this dual role. On the one hand a principal is guide and counselor, on the other perceived as judge and jury. The reasons have much to do with the teachers' professional status; the isolated nature of classroom teaching; teachers' deep-seated suspicion of interference in their instructional practice; the idiosyncratic nature of the job; practical problems associated with organizing supervision within a school; and the concern teachers feel about their ability to offer any constructive help to a colleague in difficulty. These barriers and constraints to effective supervision have often been allowed to determine both the mode and extent of supervisory practice. Supervision often relies on indirect measures of performance, or it has operated on a crisis basis. When things go wrong decisions are often made based on an insufficient amount of relevant data. Administrators commonly adopt indirect measures to appraise teacher *performance* rather than attempting to appraise classroom practice and how effectively students *learn*. Indirect indicators include the instructional program, lesson plans, and the use of examination and test results. It is not unknown for principals to use even less direct indicators such as the noise level of a classroom as perceived from the hallway or the frequency of complaints from parents as the first indications of potential concerns.

These indirect methods of supervision do not form an adequate basis for a collaborative working relationship. If teachers are to accept a greater measure of mutual accountability for their work, they must develop confidence and skills and be provided with the means to observe and influence one another within the classroom. Some form of direct observation and instructional dialogue with colleagues is necessary. One technique for meeting these requirements, called Quality Learning Circles, is discussed in Chapter 7. However, the importance of their place in the sequence of the School Development process can be briefly considered at this point. Some schools will not have developed the necessary collective knowledge, understandings, values, working relationships, and organizational structures to make Quality Learning Circles work as an innovation introduced independently of a broader school development initiative. The attributes upon which Quality Learning Circles are founded cannot be established overnight, or through brief inservicing. For most schools, consideration of Quality Learning Circles is a Phase 3 activity and should not be implemented until the preparatory work has been accomplished in the previous two phases, where the emphasis is on working together as a school.

More Effective Systems for the Assessment, Evaluation, and Appraisal of Student Progress and Instructional Programs

A current challenge for schools is to appraise their own performance. To do this effectively, they must be clear about their goals; be sure of their objectives as steps toward these goals; plan the curriculum and instructional programs which meet their objectives; appraise student progress; and, on the basis of the data gathered from these activities, review their work and make the consequential decisions for future action. But if this challenge is so clear, why do schools find it so difficult to perform their own appraisals? The answer, again, seems to relate to the organizational development of each school. Appraisal–whether of teachers, instructional programs, or students–is a demanding, threatening activity. When a school has passed through the early phases of the School Development process it will have:

- increased its collective knowledge;
- developed some of the values and relationships that evolve from collaboration;
- introduced supportive structural arrangements.

Only at this point in the developmental process will effective supervisory and appraisal procedures stand any chance of being imple-

Appraisal–whether of teachers, instructional programs, or students–is a demanding, threatening activity.

mented successfully and impact significantly on the quality of instructional programs. School, principal, and teacher appraisal is discussed fully in Part IV.

A Shift To the Norm of "Your Problem Is Our Problem"

As teachers come to a better understanding of the way the organization operates through Phase 1 of the developmental process, and as they experience more opportunities for working together and discussing common problems through Phase 2, professional isolation begins to break down. Teachers see that many problems and challenges cannot be tackled unilaterally, and that as part of a developing sense of mutual responsibility they have an obligation toward colleagues who need support. During Phases 3 and 4, principals can build on this culture of collaboration and work with the faculty, rebuilding organizational structures and teacher development initiatives that help teachers to help each other. Two case studies illustrate.

In this first example we take a look at an aspect of spelling. There are 300 or so essential words for communication that make up from one-half to three-quarters of the words the average person reads and writes. For schools the question is how students learn these words in a systematic way so that year after year they are not taught what they already know, or worse still, not getting an opportunity to learn the words they do not know. How many fourth-grade teachers are continually faced with their students writing "thay" instead of "they?" Fourth-grade teachers will say most of their number. Oak Street Elementary School fourth-grade teachers were no exception. Oak Street had moved some way toward a more collaborative culture. Its periodic staff forums were an opportunity to raise issues of a professional nature, and if a cause found support, to initiate the gathering of information about it. A fourth-grade teacher raised the matter of the number of students in her class who lacked control over these essential words in their writing.

During the discussion that followed, it was clear that a number of teachers had not considered the importance of a consistent, systematic approach to the issue, nor were they familiar with a list of such words. A first-grade teacher provided a list that she had extracted from a professional publication. It was agreed, as a first step toward understanding the issue, that a survey would be taken at each grade level, including kindergarten, from the sample list of essential words. The results were predictable. Learning was spotty, unsystematic, and inconsistent. There was no school-wide monitoring, and no overall responsibility. Teachers were making assumptions about what their colleagues were teaching that bore little relationship to what students were learning—at least as far as this aspect of spelling was concerned. The question now was what to do about it. The options were discussed at length by grade-level meetings and open forum. A consensus emerged that the learning of these words should be consistently monitored in all grades. A small team of faculty agreed to work on a proposal. The result, after further consideration of the team's report, was a list of 275 words, including some—like place names—particular to the local community. Beginning in kindergarten, each word would be highlighted by the teacher on the student's copy of the list once the student displayed evidence of having control over the word in his or her daily writing. A different color highlighter would be used each year and the list would form part of the student's assessment portfolio. The faculty also agreed that by the end of third grade, there would be a clear expectation that all students would control every word on the list. The Oak Street faculty,

The Oak Street faculty, collaboratively, had taken a mutual responsibility for an issue, where previously there was little responsibility.

collaboratively, had taken a mutual responsibility for an issue, where previously there was little responsibility. The way was open to consider similar school-wide issues.

First Avenue School, like others in its large urban district, was subject to annual standardized testing in reading at the third and fifth grades. Thus, each year the third- and fifth-grade teachers were in the spotlight, carrying the banner for the place the school achieved in the list of published test scores. One year, a batch of third-grade test scores for First Avenue slid significantly and the two teachers of the lowest scoring third graders, while not openly blamed, still felt they had let the school down. The principal's analysis of the results and the gathering of other data from the third-grade classrooms suggested that it may not have been the student's reading progress that had affected the scores as significantly as the students' preparedness for the tests. The matter was raised for discussion by the principal as a faculty issue rather than a third-grade issue. What responsibility did all teachers have to prepare students for the expectations of the third- and fifth-grade testing? What, for example, might be the things a kindergarten teacher could do to help prepare students for later testing? With the help of a team of third- and fifth-grade teachers a simple program was devised to sharpen the skills of both teachers and students in preparation for the taking of standardized tests. All teachers were held accountable for seeing that every student was prepared for the required testing. What was "your" problem was becoming "our" problem.

Greater Participation in Decisions Concerning the Allocation of Resources

There is much talk these days about shared decision making in schools. There may be less understanding about what it means in practice. For example, there are probably no school decisions more sensitive than the critical concerns of the allocation of resources and the control of that allocation. One can learn more about the true goals of a school from looking at the way it allocates its scarce resources of teachers, funding, building space, and time than can be gained from reading any number of parent handbooks or statements of school policy. Reconsidering a school's current decision-making pattern is an activity that properly falls into Phase 1 of the School Development sequence, but the structural arrangements necessary to make such decision making more effective come within Phase 3.

In this example, a new town council decided to change the way funding was allocated to the school system. Traditionally, funding had been dispersed from decisions based on the board of education's budget prepared by the school superintendent. Because this was a line item approval without the ability to transfer funds among the various categories, there was very little flexibility, even if things beyond the superintendent's control put pressure on part of the budget. The business of reallocation was cumbersome, slow, and time-consuming. With the superintendent's blessing, the board decided to push school budgeting decisions down to each school site. The schools were granted an allocation based on their previous total expenditures and required to budget for the next school year. Even special education funding, which the district had always allocated by way of salaries for special educators, was now a school budgeting responsibility.

Like her colleagues, the principal at Main Street Elementary was anticipating the change, yet somewhat apprehensive about its implications. She was given four weeks to prepare her budget for the coming school year. The implications of the new budgeting procedure for Main Street were significant since some staff loss was anticipated. To its advantage, the school had already developed good working relationships and ways of initiating faculty negotiations and decision making. First, Main Street had come a long way toward developing the structures for a tighter focus on teaching and learning. The faculty had, together, decided upon the instructional goal for the next three years that *every* student would leave Main Street a confident, competent reader and writer. Second, to reach this goal, certain objectives had been agreed to for the following year, such as every teacher being skilled in taking running records of reading behaviors, and that all teachers would make a special study of using appropriate instructional resources. These objectives alone had an implicit and substantial teacher development commitment. Another objective related to teachers meeting a wider range of student learning needs in reading instruction. This step suggested that fewer students would be referred to remediation out of the classroom. In budgeting terms this would mean a lower expenditure for certain special programs, and so on. Even so, to suggest that there would not be acrimony, frustration, even anger, is to downplay the reality of people working through difficult decisions.

The point of this case is to suggest that as part of the responsibility of allocating the school's scarce resources, the principal had to continually remind her faculty what they had already agreed to as their teaching and learning priorities. As a faculty used to data gathering and working together, negotiating the allocation of the school's resources among the priority items simply became part of the collaborative dialogue. Again, these budget decisions were difficult for Main Street. They would have been substantially more difficult if the earlier two phases of its School Development process had not been worked through.

In earlier chapters, we talked about policy makers attempting to make changes in the quality of educational achievement by changing the system's structures and forcing schools to do things differently. It was suggested that such juggling does not always achieve what is intended. The reason is now, hopefully, more apparent. Schools can change to meet a changing environment such as a new funding regime if its core values include the "habit" of gathering data and collaboratively analyzing it.

A More Explicit Negotiation of Psychological Contracts

It is only possible to develop a truly collaborative style of management through School Development if the value of pluralism is respected and fostered. Collaboration does not mean the repression of individual interests in favor of organizational ends. Nor does it mean imposing a uniform pattern of behavior on the faculty. There should always be scope for the involvement of faculty and the discussion of differences, and these differences should be discussed openly and frankly. Where some form of consistent action is called for, such as the allocation of the Main Street budget discussed above, negotiation will be required. Once again, it is the quality of the process that will be just as important as the negotiated outcome. In short:

- determining the comfort level of involvement for each teacher to commit to is a Phase 1 activity;
- negotiating and influencing colleagues in the modification of their positions while maintaining effective and professional collegial relationships is a Phase 2 activity;
- working within negotiated, "contractual" boundaries in the building of new structural arrangements is a very important part of Phase 3.

It is only possible to develop a truly collaborative style of management through School Development if the value of pluralism is respected and fostered.

School Development is a process, and the authors' experience suggests that unless this process is worked through in a deliberate and sequential manner, the "psychological contracts" on which collaborative activity is founded cannot be openly negotiated. It is not always easy for a principal to know the personal agenda of each teacher, or their professional expectations. Something about these expectations can be gleaned by asking each faculty member two questions at the beginning of each year:

- What are the three things that you expect of the school this year?
- What are the three things that you think the school expects of you?

The interesting thing about responses to these questions is that they are likely to change both in substance and tone as a school moves through the School Development process. Main Street again.

One year a faculty member had mischievously suggested "better coffee in the faculty room" in answer to the first question before suggesting more substantive expectations. However, even such a throwaway response has deeper implications about what teachers expect in their own space. In previous years, among the banter and inconsequential discourse of the faculty room, was an underlying theme. If teachers were talking about students it was generally about their behavior–their inappropriate behavior–and if given the license, what the teachers might do about it. Whether they meant it seriously or not, the way some teachers referred to their students about their lack of ability or willingness to learn actually deterred other teachers from going into the faculty room. The only time those teachers who opted out of the faculty room actually engaged with other faculty members was during the full faculty meeting which, at that time, dealt mainly with organizational matters. And, as these teachers came to expect, the very same people who dominated the faculty room did most of the talking. The net effect was a collegial environment that lacked substantial professional discussion and unwittingly supported a strong division of opinion over most issues. As this school worked through the phases of School Development, the quality of discussion gradually changed. As more and more Main Street teachers came to appreciate the value of running records (their teacher development objective) as an assessment tool for reading, the more they talked about them in casual conversation. All teachers were required to bring a running record to faculty meetings and to spend the first fifteen minutes of the meeting in mutual conversation with a colleague analyzing and proposing the next steps in instruction. Conversations about running records spilled over into faculty room discussion. These conversations had Main Street teachers expanding the boundaries of their informal professional discussion, establishing new psychological contracts about professionalism, both formally and informally.

A Closer Relationship with the Wider School Community

The relationship between a school and its immediate community is not always an easy one. Sometimes a school will adopt a relatively passive role, reacting only to the complaints and prods from the more vociferous members of the community and seeking what is perceived by some as unwelcome special or self-interest. The response of a school is often to toughen its skin and become less willing to respond, with the result that there is a growing mutual suspicion between a school and its community. In this unhappy state, the school is neither developing a

A school in which the faculty has developed clear instructional goals that are shared with its community can articulate with equal clarity its immediate objectives.

role for its community, nor is the community accepting that it can have a positive, supportive role. These are both things that need to be worked on, with the initiative inevitably with the school. A school in which the faculty has developed clear instructional goals that are shared with its community can articulate with equal clarity its immediate objectives. It can also offer a curriculum and instructional program that is consistent, and it is well placed to meet its part of the bargain of working toward achieving those shared community goals. A school that has genuinely expanded the amount of influence its members can use has many more options available to it. Such a school need not wait until community opinion is fully resolved on an issue. If it is developing a positive, collaborative, working relationship with its community similar to the relationship developing among the members of its faculty, it can seek to influence that opinion. Its influence can be positive when it is aligned to the broad understandings that the principal and faculty share. Southpark School offers an example of developing good working relationships with its community.

The Southpark community is typical of many suburban school districts. A mixed community, it had some parents who held strong opinions on most things and who were not at all reluctant to share them. Southpark Elementary was approached by such a parent group, who felt that their children were not learning to read or write. In the parents' opinion, the students were not developing the skills of reading or writing and needed "more phonics." Essentially, the problem appeared to have arisen from students taking home draft writing that appeared full of "mistakes," and from students being allowed, as one parent put, to "invent" their spelling. As a solution, the parent group urged the school to adopt a phonics-based program. There was no hint to the principal that there was any room for compromise. The first reaction of the principal was to become defensive–to defend his leadership, the faculty, the school's reading and writing curriculum, and the instructional program. He resolved only to listen, to investigate the parents' complaint, to consider the proposed program, and to hold a future meeting at which he would report back to the parent group. The most disquieting inference from the initial episode with this group of parents was the fact that they were willing–indeed, eager–to approach the school and demand that the school do their bidding. What of other parents? How many were ready to fall silently in behind this group of opinion leaders by supporting frustrations or misunderstandings about what the school was trying to do? Before raising the matter with the faculty, the principal developed his own course of action. He needed data about the students the group of parents represented. He needed data on the instructional programs currently offered in reading and writing. After the faculty had gathered the data and discussed them together, it was proposed that there should be an open meeting with parents to reconfirm the school's goals for literacy teaching and learning and how those goals were being pursued. The issue, the faculty agreed, was not one of "invented spelling" but of supporting students learning to spell through the use of their spelling approximations. The problem was one of communication and how the school had to continue to involve parents in what the school was trying to do. The principal's strategy was directed toward improving the school's communication with parents, not blindly defending the status quo.

Collaborative action requires a working consensus on the major policies and instructional programs of the school.

A Commitment to Cooperate

Collaborative action, by definition, requires a working consensus on the major policies and instructional programs of the school. The term "working consensus" means that participants in a discussion on an issue are willing to suspend their judgment in order that a decision be made. Consensus does not mean total unanimity on those decisions. Schools are pluralistic institutions, and it is unlikely that there will be total agreement among the faculty on any proposal for significant change. It is helpful to develop decision-making guidelines as a Phase 3 outcome. Using these guidelines for coming to consensus, all of the important issues can be thoroughly debated. Data would be collected and analyzed and all points of view have the opportunity to be canvassed. When the time comes to make a decision, all the parties to that agreement, whether for or against the final decision, will be required to abide by it. At the very least, those who oppose an agreed course of action will undertake not to sabotage the efforts of their colleagues. The interests of the dissenting minority will be safeguarded by a formal commitment to review the group decision by a certain date. This kind of nonsabotage commitment is absolutely necessary when a school is considering new structural arrangements during Phase 3, or beginning to implement significant changes to the instructional programs during Phase 4. The principal is the keyholder to this agreement. Few innovations will succeed against the efforts of a group of teachers determined to resist, perhaps even to derail, them. For example, a move to reallocate duties among members of the faculty is threatened if teachers who have long had a role in which status and power are embedded are resistant. The loss of this perceived individual status and authority must somehow be replaced by the satisfaction gained through greater collaboration and the common good that accrues. Unless a school has gone through some of the experiences of Phases 1 and 2 of the School Development process and embraces a genuine collaborative working culture, no principal should assume that it will be possible to reach decisions on contentious issues through a shared decision making or a consensus approach.

The Principal's Role in the School Development Process

To conclude this part, it may be useful to review the role of the reflective principal in the process of school development. The stance of the administrator is a critical variable throughout the School Development process. Opportunities for shared work, analysis, and the evaluation of understandings and of practices and policies have to be created. Risk-taking and lateral thinking need to be encouraged and supported. The development of a set of norms for collaboration can only be successful if the principal shows through active support that further development of the School Development process is being encouraged. There needs to be opportunity for discussion about specific instructional and supervisory practices, opportunity for mutual observation, time for joint preparation of instructional programs, and time for teacher development activity. Despite intuitive doubts, by encouraging increased participation a principal does not give up power; instead, *a larger amount of influence is created.* This can only enrich the process, since influence is informed by both data and their analyses.

Teachers' attitudes to School Development will be determined by their own experience of it through their personal and professional development; by the relationships they develop with their colleagues; by the level of commitment it engenders to their classroom programs; by the level of cohesion they experience among their faculty; and by the opportunities they have to influence decisions they consider important to them. It is the principal's role to ensure that the increasing

It is the principal's role to ensure that the increasing collaboration of Phase 2 is a constructive and optimistic experience that will maintain the momentum through the School Development cycle.

collaboration of Phase 2 is a constructive and optimistic experience that will maintain the momentum through the School Development cycle.

To reinforce the crucial importance of each phase in the developmental process, the four phases are restated below in the form of broad questions.

Phase 1. How Do Things Work Around Here?

The only way to answer the question "how do things work around here?" is to gather data related to how things really work. Ask any number of teachers in a typical school how decisions are made there and the possibility is that there will be any number of different responses, but those responses in themselves are valuable data. They tell the inquirer a lot about the way things are seen to work. Through this data-gathering phase, leadership activities will include:

- clarifying key issues that face the faculty and the wider school community;
- supporting the faculty in the development of data-gathering skills;
- facilitating the decision-making process about priorities for data gathering;
- supporting data gathering;
- managing the data-reporting processes;
- providing access to professional periodicals and other resources and people;
- encouraging discussion about people's experiences.

Phase 2. Can We Start Looking at Our Problems Together?

The advantages of collaboration and mutual responsibility have already been discussed. The key point is that a school is an environment in which a number of people come together for a common purpose. Problems or issues do not belong only to those who create or raise them. They are shared by the school community. Their resolution is best approached by working together. During this phase of collaborative analysis, as the faculty learns to work together, leadership activities will include:

- extending the range of collaborative skills through interactive training;
- monitoring the level of faculty and community participation;
- supporting an open approach to discussion about collected data;
- encouraging the exchange of experiences through classroom observation, visiting speakers, and other opportunities to consider the school's issues;
- offering support to encourage professional conversations about key issues;
- continually providing summary reviews about the school's progress.

This kind of leadership is the *process facilitator*. As a school's development moves into the next phases it becomes important for the principal to interpret for the faculty the changes in the way the school is becoming a learning organization. In this sense the school begins to think about changes to its structural qualities as a result of its ability to work together, when the process of collaborating itself determines the changes to its shape.

Phase 3. Will We Need to Make Changes to the Way the School is Organized?

The gathering of data and the collaborative analysis may lead to obvious conclusions about how the organizational structures within the

The School Development process turns to teachers' understandings about teaching and learning, and to their classroom practice.

school need to change. For example, if teachers are unsure of how decisions are made, or have different perceptions of the decision-making process, there will be a need to consider new decision-making structures that offer all faculty members the opportunity to participate. In this way the process keeps coming back on itself. Teachers need to participate to share the analysis of data. To participate they need to reshape the decision-making structures from data they have discussed about an existing framework. A school does not "do" School Development. The School Development process is a way a school gets itself to continually work better. The principal becomes the *collector of artifacts*. As structural changes are contemplated in Phase 3, it is important that the school community be continually reminded about "what we currently do well," despite the focus on issues, challenges, and problems; the trade-offs in any decision and how they need to be considered before changes are decided upon; the progress that has been achieved toward the school development objectives; the value to increasing student achievement in this progress; and that the school's mission provides the direction for continuing school development.

Phase 4. Are We Now Able to Concentrate on Teaching and Learning?

Teaching and learning is, after all, the business of the school. It is the reason why time and commitment are invested in the School Development process. For a principal, the focus is establishing a commitment from the school community to this sequence, then actively facilitating and leading each of the phases in a cyclic and continuous way. Through Phase 4, the School Development process turns to teachers' understandings about teaching and learning, and to their classroom practice. Teacher development becomes school development through a faculty and school community whose sense of working together is the foundation for a community of learners. This is a critical phase for the principal, one in which educational leadership is expressed more directly by the changes being made to the way teachers work in their classrooms. In this phase the principal's activities include:

- supporting with the faculty a clarification of the community's curriculum expectations;
- the development of consistent understandings about critical aspects of teaching and learning such as reading and writing;
- developing curriculum benchmarks through the grades;
- supporting teachers in their mutual observations of classroom practice;
- encouraging continual professional dialogue and discussion among the faculty;
- the further gathering of data on issues about teaching and learning arising from a faculty that is continually refining its understanding and practice.

Part III

Individual Development

Part III

Individual Development

At the end of Part I the authors proposed a matrix for analyzing the development tasks facing a school wishing to become a more effective and collaborative learning community. A distinction was drawn between developmental and appraisal activities on the one hand, and individual and school-wide activities on the other. This part moves from the school-wide or large group focus to concentrating on the individual development of principals and teachers.

It may seem unusual to consider the school at an organizational level before considering its individual members. The Development Matrix is worked through in this order because most schools will find it necessary to make some progress on school-wide development activities before they will win the commitment of the faculty to the individual development activities discussed here. Faculty members working together on their professional development need first to learn to work together. And similarly, readers may find the approach taken in this part makes more sense against the background of the previous part than it would if the order were reversed.

The theme of Part III is the simple but ambitious task of improving the quality of teaching and learning. Chapter 6 explores the title theme of this book–how principals and teachers can engage in a process of sustained *reflection* on classroom teaching and learning. Chapter 7 suggests two approaches, Quality Learning Circles and Thematic Supervision, that principals might select to help a school channel and direct that reflection in positive and effective ways.

Chapter 6

The Reflective Process

The educational profession faces insistent demands to "get it right." While economists are virtually unanimous in suggesting that a sluggish economy is the result of long-term shifts in world trade, politicians are frequently tempted to look to the school systems for quick-fix solutions. There is an impatience with the unpredictability and the imprecision of the schooling process, and a determination to make schools more productive and more accountable to public expectations. Any measure that seems to offer a reliable technique for delivering desired learning outcomes becomes attractive.

The technical "teacher proofing" of the school curriculum, for example, is a vestige of what Schlechty referred to as the school operating as a factory. This approach has a certain appeal to policy makers who view learning as a passive process of knowledge acquisition and teaching as a technical task with requirements that can be precisely and reliably identified. There is an associated belief that there are some universal and consistent techniques teachers should use to accomplish these ends. The introduction of some form of a teacher appraisal system, the argument goes, will ensure that teachers apply approved techniques and should ensure more effective schools.

There is a growing understanding that schools will maximize student learning by providing a best fit between what teachers do, students' experiences, and the ways the students learn.

This reductionist view of teaching is becoming increasingly untenable in the light of research on effective teaching and learning (Smyth 1988). In its place there is a growing understanding that schools will maximize student learning by providing a best fit between what teachers do, students' experiences, and the ways the students learn. The challenge of teaching is not to follow a standard set of teaching strategies for all students, but to decide on the appropriate teaching response to any particular learning challenge. This involves teachers and administrators in *thinking about what they do as they do it*. This "reflection," as it is increasingly called, is a critical component of effective practice.

Donald Schön has defined this reflective process and the theory of knowledge upon which it is based (Schön 1983). Schön makes a crucial distinction between "objective knowledge" and "knowledge-in-action." Objective knowledge includes scientifically verifiable principles of teaching and learning that a teacher or an administrator can rely on to hold good in any given set of circumstances. Schön claims that such knowledge is seldom available in a teaching and learning situation. Instead, teachers engage in a constant process of reflecting on what is happening and how their actions are affecting the learning situation. He calls this process "knowledge-in-action" (Smyth 1988, 167).

As they are teaching, teachers think about the progress that is being achieved and the meanings that are being developed by the class. They adjust both the content and the process of their teaching as a result. The final form of the learning sequence may bear little resemblance to the teacher's initial lesson plan. Similar knowledge-in-action takes place when principals are engaged in professional conversations with individuals or groups. Decisions about the course of the conversation are made as the conversation proceeds rather than being planned thoroughly in advance. This reflection-in-action may result in the principal changing his or her beliefs and understandings in a particular context.

This concept of reflection is not new in the field of education. John Dewey (1933) explored similar ideas and wrote of reflection as a specialized form of thinking. The process he described, beginning with doubt and concern and leading through focused inquiry to rational response, included the concept that is central to Schön's basic argument. This is "the paradox that one cannot know without acting and one cannot act without knowing" (Grimmett, Rostad, and Ford 1988, 6).

> The function of reflective thought is, therefore, to transform a situation in which there is experienced obscurity, doubt, conflict, disturbance of some sort, into a situation that is clear, coherent, settled, harmonious (Dewey 1933, 100–101).

To be reflective in a teaching and learning context is to consider a range of possible actions before moving to the next stage of the episode, or before responding to class initiatives. This will often occur within a short time frame, and to be successful requires the teacher to be able to hold in his or her mind a suitable range of possible options. In many situations teachers will need to explore some of these with the students, withholding judgment until it becomes clear in which direction it would be most profitable for the episode to continue. In this sense reflection is a kind of interactive reasoning. This reasoning will be heavily dependent on the inputs and prior learning of students, but will always contain an unpredictable element.

This emphasis on reflection is consistent

To be reflective in a teaching and learning context is to consider a range of possible actions before moving to the next stage.

with the "professional" view of supervision discussed earlier and is at odds with the "bureaucratic" view. That is, a reflective view of teaching
would maintain that growth in teacher effectiveness is more likely to occur when small groups of
teachers are provided with opportunities to
reflect with each other on a regular basis, rather
than being pressed to incorporate a set range of
so-called "competencies" into their practice.
Through regular interaction with each other they
will widen the range of options open to them;
they will gain insights into situations deemed
dilemmas by their peers; and they will have an
opportunity to reflect on their own work by discussing their practice and their beliefs about that
practice with their colleagues. Understandings of
teaching derived from the intuitive endeavors of
teachers can be just as important as knowledge
derived from scientific inquiry. Reflection is normally an unstructured, intuitive process.

If reflection is to become the focus for school-
based teacher development—which is the principal thesis of this book—it will need to become
more explicit, structured, and shared. John
Smyth (1989) suggests that one step in this
process is for teachers to structure their reflection by asking themselves the following questions:

- What do I do? (Describe)
- What does this mean? (Inform)
- How did I come to be like this? (Confront)
- How might I do things differently? (Recon-
  struct)

Describing

Descriptions can range from formal diary
keeping to more informal "telling of stories" or
writing metaphors that encompass the knowledge, beliefs, and understandings that teachers

think lie behind the series of events that they wish to address. Teachers frequently talk with one another about their classroom work. Much of this talk takes the form of anecdotes and stories. Illustrating a real event with a metaphor to add impact and meaning to the illustration is sometimes useful.

Informing

Once a teacher has described what it is he or she does, or what he or she believes, it is then possible to analyze that description and begin to deduce the theoretical base on which these actions or beliefs are founded. For example, a teacher might be thinking about the rules and procedures within the classroom and how such routines impinge on teaching and learning strategies. If there are many restrictions about when and to whom students may talk, then an assumption could be made that teacher talk is many times more valuable than student talk. In other words, the teacher is working from a personal theory that all students will learn effectively by listening carefully to the teacher.

Confronting

The next step in the process is confrontation, when the teacher asks "How did I come to be like this?" Smyth (1989, 7) proposes a further set of questions at this point:

- What do my classroom practices say about my assumptions, values, and beliefs about teaching and learning?
- Where did these ideas come from?
- What social practices are expressed in these ideas?

- What is it that causes me to maintain my theories?
- What views of power do they embody?
- Whose interests seem to be served by my practices?
- What is it that acts to constrain my views of what is possible in teaching and learning?

Reconstructing

The future possible action phase or "reconstructing" element then follows. Many events influencing students and many of their individual characteristics are outside the control of teachers and schools. A reflective approach accepts this fact and focuses on improving the quality of teaching and learning for which teachers are responsible through the process of interactive reasoning, both alone and with others.

The Reflective Principal

In applying the notion of reflection to the work of the principal it is necessary to appreciate that scientific understanding of administrative behavior is scarcely more advanced than an understanding of teacher behavior. More than half a century of research into organizational behavior has produced few empirically validated solutions that principals can use to meet the challenges of their work. The solutions that have been forthcoming tend to address matters of a trivial or routine nature. Even the commonly used management theories are of limited value to the manager seeking specific guidance, and often have conflicting implications for practice.

Rational actions can be said to spring from a logical examination of the relevant facts. Lying behind such an examination, however, is a range of personal theories about the nature of learning, about how organizations work, and about personal motivation, to mention just a few. A reflective approach involves acknowledging and perhaps uncovering these personal theories and making them explicit (Griffiths and Tann 1992). This is not a simple, straightforward task. It requires principals to commit some of their professional time to developing the role of researcher. Principals could well begin by noting and recording the language they use on a day-to-day basis to describe and develop their work. They should then examine the imagery of their language in order to relate the metaphors they use to the personal theories that they hold. For example, do they describe their role as:

- the captain of the ship;
- a guide for travelers;
- a custodian of knowledge;
- the leader of the community?

Can an exploration of these images help in understanding and expanding the theoretical viewpoints that lie behind the images? In the view of Griffiths and Tann (1992), this can be difficult, as the personal theories contained within the metaphors are usually small scale and particular, whereas the more general theory, which they call "public theory," is large scale and universal.

The following examples of reflection in action begin with a teacher at the Vale School. She tells a story about her own personal and professional development and the issue of her appraisal by the principal. This example is followed by another in which the principal discusses with his colleagues the same issues from a different perspective, and how the options for action arose from their collective reflection.

A reflective approach involves acknowledging and perhaps uncovering these personal theories and making them explicit (Griffiths and Tann 1992).

A Teacher's Story About Her Own Learning

The faculty of Vale School established Quality Learning Circles as a form of regular professional conversations to share their instructional approaches with faculty colleagues. This example of a professional development initiative is explored more fully in the next chapter. Quality Learning Circles provide opportunities for teachers to discuss approaches to teaching and learning across the grade levels rather than only with other teachers at the same grade level. The sessions were enjoyed and popular, replacing one full faculty meeting each month.

At the same time, under a district mandate, the principal was required to introduce a system of formal teacher appraisal. While the faculty was committed to the idea of sharing and discussing examples of each other's practice, the new district mandate raised questions about a possible conflict between the purposes of professional development and the requirements for teacher appraisal. In her story, the teacher put the issue this way:

I believe that the major purpose of a teacher appraisal system must be to improve teaching and learning. To do this for me as a teacher, it is important that I identify the ways that the level of my teaching and the level of my students' learning can be raised. In other words, appraisal should be providing insights into my current practice that will encourage me to improve it, rather than simply assuring the district that I am working at a minimum level of competence and deserving of continued employment and my paycheck.

Our Quality Learning Circles have given a whole new direction to my work and the appraising of my work. When I attend these meetings I am constantly thinking about what goes on in my own room as I listen to the others talk about theirs. So many of the dilemmas and problems are so similar to mine. What is surprising are the different explanations for our common issues and the different understandings and thoughts we have about them. These so often vary from my own. Recently Susan was talking about how discussion was managed in her room. She was questioning an insistence that children raise their hands before talking and how this was inhibiting much of their learning. She talked about the data she had gathered and the interpretations that she had made. I was beginning to feel quite uncomfortable. I had never questioned whether or not this was good for students' learning. Raising hands before talking was something I did as a student and that I have always insisted my students do. After the session and talking with other teachers I discovered that a number of us had similar beliefs. The "raising hands" issue became a topic of faculty conversation over the next little while. Jennifer, the fourth-grade teacher, brought some articles to our next meeting that suggested some alternative approaches for students participating in classroom discussions. Ann, who had joined our staff recently, mentioned that she had some groups working in her room who were "listening with their eyes," and who had quite well-developed procedures for ensuring that everyone took part in a conversation without signaling their intention by raising hands. She invited us to visit her room. John talked about our own discussion group and how we had never felt the need to raise hands among ourselves. He asked us to think about the transition from student to adult discussion. What was different about adult conversations, and what are the indicators that might suggest a class or group is ready to participate in discussion without the need to raise hands?

This whole topic had given me a great deal to think about. Yet, I had a problem when our principal joined the group. He became very interested and fully participated in the discussion, but I had a nagging doubt about sharing my own uncertainties. To what extent was my uncertainty going to be a factor in the appraisal process? If I was trying a different approach in my instruction and it was not going so well, what was the principal going to take from this in terms of my competence? Put another way, does just thinking about these issues suggest that I am not competent–or is it that I still have much to learn? I would like to think that appraising my classroom practice, the principal sees me as a learner. It is that willingness to continually learn that I think is important in teacher appraisal.

The Teacher's Metaphor

In trying to describe this idea of being a learner–her process of teacher development–this teacher suggested that their discussion group was like being a member of a jazz band. Each member of the group knew and trusted each other and was familiar with the discussion's routines. The staging was agreed upon and each member was committed to the performance. In one sense there was a "musical sequence" and an "underlying melody." What was surprisingly similar to the jazz band, she explained, was the verve and creativity that individuals brought to their group. Their solo offerings built on what had just gone before and in a sense were "rehearsed" at previous meetings. She noted how many of these "performances" brought smiles to everyone's faces and how members silently applauded. There were also, she said, the subtle shades and tones that others had used to influence her own presentations, and the experience was enhanced, she concluded, by their enjoyment of each other and their mutual interdependence.

I am now constantly thinking about what I am doing and why I am doing it.

The Teacher's Reflection

The teacher continued her explanation:

Most often it is the simple but subtle things I hear in the stories of others that most influence my thinking and teaching. We all enjoy the cut and thrust of the discussion, particularly the "So what does it mean?" phase. As a group we often use the form "It seems as if..." when we try to answer the question "How did I come to be like this?" or "Why am I instructing in this way?" What we talk about very often gives me pause to reconsider, and provides a spur for thinking about the options I have for doing things differently.

This new thinking is not always what I had planned to consider and the goals I achieve are not always the goals I planned to reach. Does this mean that I am being inconsistent; that I am really not sure about my job? Probably not. I think I am struggling toward greater consistency in my thinking, in my understandings about teaching and learning, and in my classroom practice. I am now constantly thinking about what I am doing and why I am doing it, and that means I am prepared to try things differently. This is really making a difference to what I actually do in the classroom, and what my students are learning. Surely, this commitment to reflecting on my practice is the most important thing in my appraisal as a teacher.

Meaningful Narrative

Composing the narrative invokes reflection for the storyteller, and trying to use a metaphor encourages a clearer construction of the issues. This is what is meant by giving teachers *voice*—not simply giving time for a general discussion in a full faculty meeting, but rather constructing a framework where colleagues can share their classroom practices and attempt to explain how their practices are consistent with their beliefs about teaching and learning. They use illustrations from their own practices that can be shared by their colleagues wrestling with the same issues as an integral part of their classroom lives. Sometimes it is the way that the story is told that needs to be refocused, but once accepted, the discussion generated by the reflective questions and comments from others in the group will also become more focused and relevant. Narrative constructed in this way can reinforce the value of existing effective practice, can alert teachers to other approaches for meeting their own challenges, and can provide a solid basis for constructive group analysis of teaching and learning. Nonetheless, an issue still remains for a principal. How can the needs for this kind of teacher development be reconciled with the requirement for teacher appraisal?

The Principal's Story: Describing

Following a leadership seminar in the Vale School District a group of principals decided to form their own discussion group. It was based around the same principles as the Quality Learning Circles. The main purpose of the group was to facilitate and deepen their reflective practice. They agreed that they would meet once a month and take turns presenting a narrative that illustrated some important part of their work. They also agreed to focus closely on the narrative and to work through one "story" at a time. Gerald, the principal of Vale School, shared the faculty's recent experience:

At Vale we are now using one out of every four of our regular full faculty meetings to talk about our understandings about teaching and learning which guide and inform our classroom practice. Each faculty member forms part of a group of five or six colleagues. As the trust has grown in these groups, the faculty are sharing some of their fundamental thinking about the nature of what they do. Recently, one of the teachers thought that the classroom convention of raising hands before contributing may be inhibiting students learning from each other. The issue was talked about in two or three sessions, including discussion on the results of observations teachers had made in one another's classrooms. Partway through this discussion, I felt my participation in the group was being challenged. Two of the teachers suggested that under the recent district mandate about teacher appraisal, my participation as a member of the discussion group could be compromised by my using what was discussed in these conversations in judging teacher competence. Would I not be questioning teachers' effectiveness because they were openly sharing their uncertainties about their classroom practice? If they were going to try different approaches, what if they were not successful?

The dual role of the principal as developer and appraiser is a dilemma faced by every principal.

The Principals' Discussion: Informing

Gerald and his colleagues discussed the issue at length. The dual role of the principal as developer and appraiser is a dilemma faced by every principal. During the discussion they raised the following questions:

- Should we join groups of teachers who are sharing their uncertainties and openly discussing how their classrooms work?
- Is the principal always seen to be in an appraisal role, even when the faculty is discussing professional issues?
- If the principal remains a member of the group, will the quality of stories change to reflect the presence of the appraiser?

Throughout this part of the discussion the principals' group was able to keep a tight focus on Gerald's story. Each member of the group understood and reminded each other that this was not the time to indulge in similar stories, but rather to consider the deeper implications of the meanings contained in the story they had heard.

Questions to Gerald: Confronting

There is a very real sense in which the questions asked as part of this process helps the questioner clarify his or her own thinking as much as it requires the person being questioned–in this case Gerald–to clarify his or hers. These are the questions that Gerald's colleagues posed:

- Why is it important for you to be part of these discussion groups?
- How is your membership going to support your teachers' further professional development when they think you are continually appraising them?

- Doesn't your presence influence their ability to be open and frank with each other, the very heart of the group's purpose?

Gerald's response was thoughtful:

I am really interested in the way that we, as a faculty, think about teaching and learning. Being part of the discussion with small groups of faculty gives me a unique opportunity to hear them talk about their ideas. As a couple of the teachers implied, rather than making judgments, I'm constantly comparing what they are saying with the way I think about my own work. I know from what the teachers say, this is what others in the group do as well. It's the "thinking as you are acting" that has always attracted me. It occurred to me that this process could be an important part of teacher appraisal, but I am not sure how to make the connection. It seems to me very important that as principals we accept the fact that teachers are at different places with their own personal and professional development and that appraisal is about the extent to which they attempt to achieve their own developmental goals.

Options for Action: Gerald's Reconstruction

Implicit in Gerald's response are further questions:

- What are the options that I have, and how might I do things differently so that I can still remain part of the faculty discussion groups?
- How can I be responsible for the faculty's professional development yet, at the same time, appraise their performance as teachers?

Principals are unlikely to find recipes or scientific truths which they can apply reliably and universally to the situations presented to them.

In the end, and as a group, the principals had suggested that it was possible to fulfill a dual role—developer and appraiser. Gerald took from the discussion the possibility that appraisal could be based on the extent to which each teacher met his or her own developmental goals. The fact that they were successful or not seemed less important than the knowledge of where they were as professionals, and the extent to which they were prepared, with the support and guidance of their colleagues and their principal, to take their next step. Appraisal became the process of determining the level of the platform for their next developmental step, and being able to describe in considerable detail where they were in the process, the objective they set themselves, and the extent to which they were achieving it.

Levels of Reflection

Gerald and his colleagues also became aware that the process of *reflection* can operate on at least the following three levels:

- the simplest is at the technical or action level, where the focus is on what actually happened and what was done;
- a second level addresses the underlying assumptions that may lie behind the action, the educational goals that were selected, and the alternative goals that were discarded;
- a third level includes the moral and ethical issues involved in the episode and their social, political, and economic implications (Griffiths and Tann 1992, 77).

Schön (1987) suggests a fourth dimension of *reflection-in-action*. This is where reflection is taking place while the action is actually occurring. Principals are unlikely to find recipes or, as was stated earlier, scientific truths, which they can apply reliably and universally to the situations presented to them. When they do find theories to guide their practices, events will have a tendency to unfold contrary to these theories. A reflective stance allows considered action to continue in spite of this absence of universal theory, and personal theoretical notions can be trialed and incorporated along the way. These personal theories can then be made explicit and contestable within the school community.

A Final Reflection

What has been described here is an ideal process of individual and group reflection using members of the faculty and the principal at Vale School as an example. There is a sense in which group reflection has some parallels with a process of meditation—or even a regime of weight loss. Many individuals express occasional interest in meditation, and probably more in losing weight, but few are sufficiently strong-minded enough to continue with the regime of commitment without others of a like mind to provide mutual support and practice. It is the same with the process of reflection. Most teachers and principals benefit from the kinds of peer support that reinforces and strengthens the reflective process. School Development can provide a structure of support and reinforcement by building in the expectation that teachers and administrators will be reflecting on their practice on a continuing basis, and that this process will be a shared, collegial one. In the following chapters some of these ideas are developed further.

Chapter 7

Quality Learning Circles and Thematic Supervision

The most difficult but probably the most important challenge facing school leaders is the improvement of the quality of classroom teaching and learning. There are many indirect ways of achieving such an improvement. Improvements in teacher training, reforms in hiring, promotion and retention policies, new curricula, and the use of alternative teaching and learning media are just a few of the approaches that are commonly used. It is very easy to invest a great deal of energy and resources into such interventions without seeing measurable improvement in classroom teaching and student learning. The only obvious alternative to such indirect measures is direct supervision—observing a teacher in action, providing feedback, and discussing ways in which the teacher's classroom practices might be improved.

The most common approach to supervision over the past couple of decades or more has been a procedure variously called "in-class supervision," "clinical supervision," and "in-class support." Here a supervisor, most commonly an administrator, spends short periods of time observing a teacher, collecting data on predeter-

The most difficult but probably the most important challenge facing school leaders is the improvement of the quality of classroom teaching and learning.

mined aspects of classroom behavior, then reporting that data to the teacher. This procedure is designed to assist the observed teacher in analyzing what has taken place and to develop some conclusions about the observed behavior. This approach developed from the early work of people such as Michael Cogan (1973) and Robert Goldhammer et al. (1980), and was promoted strongly in an earlier publication by two of the authors (Prebble and Stewart 1981).

In-class supervision is based on the assumption that change in teacher behavior will come about as teachers are confronted with data about what is really going on in their classrooms. Teaching is a self-reinforcing activity, and in the normal course of events teachers seldom get an opportunity to gain an objective view of their performance. In-class supervision provides that opportunity. More specifically, there are a number of operational assumptions that underlie in-class supervision:

- teachers can be assisted to identify weaknesses in their own techniques;
- teachers will then be able and willing to demonstrate these problems to the observer;
- supervisors will suppress any of their own biases and preferences about teaching style;
- the observers have the ability to accurately record what is happening, and are also able to communicate this accurately to the teachers at a later time;
- teachers will not deliberately alter their behavior while the observers are in the classroom;
- these observations will lead to teacher improvement.

It is clear from the published studies about clinical supervision that those schools that have persisted with this approach can increase the effectiveness of teaching and learning. It is also apparent that many teachers engaged in the process of in-class supervision find the whole experience essentially negative and threatening. They particularly resist the constant focus on weaknesses and shortcomings in their teaching. Throughout the school year teachers are continually expected to identify weaknesses in their teaching techniques. The assumption is that there is always room for improvement and by using this interactive process their teaching practice will steadily improve. While most teachers would concede that there are aspects of their teaching that could be improved, the process of supervision seems to commit them to a never-ending round of observations that invariably focus on their weaknesses. It is hardly surprising that many teachers become disenchanted with the whole procedure and eventually see it only as a necessary part of the appraisal process that is required by their district or state. Supervisory visits then become nothing more than the teacher putting on a performance for the administrator in order to be seen in the best possible light.

In-class supervision, when carried through as intended, is also a technique that places great demands on the supervisor to remain objective and nonintrusive. By convention, this approach obliges the supervisor to accept the problem areas identified by the teacher under supervision even when there may be more pressing and obvious shortcomings in the latter's classroom behavior. It also requires the supervisor to ignore any behavior that lies outside the negotiated focus of concern, and to allow the teacher under observation to arrive at his or her own analysis of what is taking place. These expectations are important elements of the contract the two parties enter into, and when these expectations are not met the whole process quickly becomes discredited.

In-class supervision has been given a fair trial in many schools, and it must now be conceded that it is not an adequate vehicle for long-term faculty or school development. This period

Quality Learning Circles provide one example of how faculties can work together with a focus on teaching and learning.

of trial has revealed a number of aspects of supervision that are valuable and should be retained, as well as those aspects that are ultimately unworkable. The elements of value include:

- opportunities for teachers to observe *each other's* practice on a regular basis;
- deliberate focus on a narrow range of classroom behavior;
- the challenge to discuss aspects of practice and observations with one's colleagues in a supportive way.

The unacceptable and unworkable aspects of in-class supervision include:

- the problem-centered nature of the process;
- the requirement for teachers to identify a never-ending stream of difficulties in their classroom practice.

The authors have developed two concepts or techniques to retain the useful features of in-class supervision while abandoning the less helpful aspects. These are concepts referred to in the previous chapter: Quality Learning Circles and Thematic Supervision.

Quality Learning Circles

Quality Learning Circles provide one example of how faculties can work together with a focus on teaching and learning. David Stewart and Tom Prebble have been encouraging principals to implement this approach over many years. They have used the term *Quality Learning Circles* to emphasize the following characteristics of these groups:

- *Quality*—a goal of most schools will be to improve the quality of teaching and learning that they offer. These groups focus on those qualitative aspects;

- *Learning*—schools should be learning communities where all members–teachers, parents, and students–wish to participate in the learning process as part of their own development;
- *Circles*—schools should be collaborative enterprises where knowledge and expertise are shared and problems are solved cooperatively.

Quality Learning Circles is one method that can bring these three objectives together in a process that unites and invigorates the life of the school. Quality Learning Circles are small groups of teachers who, together, develop their professional practice. They are formed by groups of faculty who are comfortable working with each other, who represent a cross section of teachers within the school at different stages in their careers, and who also cross student age, grade, and specialist boundaries. The size of Quality Learning Circle groups should not exceed five or six teachers and they should remain intact for at least the duration of the school year. Quality Learning Circles become the basic units for individual professional development within the school. They meet regularly, preferably once a week, for at least a half hour. Their purpose is to allow teachers to study and discuss their professional practice with a group of colleagues in a supportive and nonthreatening environment. Quality Learning Circles are structured opportunities for teachers to reflect on their own professional practice and that of their colleagues. Teachers who participate in Quality Learning Circles are demonstrating that as well as teachers, they are willing learners.

Principals should join Quality Learning Circles for a time as participating members. The size of the school will determine the length of time the principal will remain with any particular group. During membership of any one group principals

The complexity and the subtlety of teaching and learning means that teachers often find it difficult to be analytical about what they observe or what they think they are doing.

have a unique and important opportunity to discuss their philosophy and their vision for schooling, to participate in the teaching and observation processes, and to demonstrate their willingness to be learners.

Quality Learning Circles could operate in a variety of ways, but typically they will follow a three-stage sequence of steps:

- the members of the group discuss a selected theme and talk about their own interpretation of that theme in their classroom teaching;
- the group members get an opportunity to observe each other demonstrating their interpretation of that theme in their teaching;
- the group discusses and reflects on what members have seen and discovered in their own and their colleagues' teaching.

Using this process teachers are able to construct new meanings and understandings to apply to their own classroom practice.

The first stage involves discussion of a selected theme. In-class supervision focused on problems that an individual teacher had identified in his or her teaching practice. These problems then provided a theme for discussion and observation between the teacher and his or her supervisor. With a larger group forming the Quality Learning Circle, it becomes necessary to select a theme that will be meaningful to the whole group. The selection of the group theme is discussed later, but for the moment assume that the group will adopt a theme and take opportunities to reflect upon it.

The complexity and the subtlety of teaching and learning means that teachers often find it difficult to be analytical about what they observe or what they think they are doing. Sometimes they will present textbook explanations that bear little resemblance to the realities of the process; or they may describe their classroom practice as if this were some sort of statement of purpose. The challenge is to get behind these taken-for-granted statements of theory or practice and encourage teachers to reflect with fresh eyes on what they are really doing and trying to do. Any attempt to provide a simple cause-and-effect analysis of what is happening will almost certainly fail to tell the whole story. However, storytelling is often a good place to begin. A group of teachers talking about their classroom work with each other can be encouraged to summarize their interpretation of the theme with a story or a metaphor. This can be a simple but powerful way to get a new perspective on what is going on. Teaching is about exchanging ideas and concepts and facilitating the construction of new and different meanings by the learner. It is not an activity that can be readily measured or quantified. While it may be possible to record and analyze the teacher's behavior, it is not easy to determine the effect that the episode is having on each member of the class. Also, the affective dimension of teaching is important, but not one that is easily assessed. Sometimes a raised eyebrow or an encouraging smile can be more significant in determining the success or failure of a teaching episode than the quality or form of the information being presented or the carefully followed lesson plan. Quality Learning Circles begin when groups of teachers tell stories to each other about how they teach, about classroom culture, and about the successes and worries of their current class group.

The second stage involves teachers visiting each other's classrooms at predetermined times to observe their colleagues putting into practice something they have discussed during the first stage. The visitor has an altogether different status and purpose from the supervisor in the in-class supervision situation. Here the observer is a learner who has come to observe something the teacher wants to share, rather than an observer coming to gather data on an area of professional weakness. If it is appropriate, and if data will help the process, the visitor gathers and uses the examples in the discussion that follows.

The third stage involves conversations between the observing teacher and the demonstrating teacher. The visitor discusses his or her understanding and interpretation with the demonstrating teacher based on the observations. The demonstrating teacher may be asked to clarify aspects of the lesson or of the underlying objectives. Following these private conversations the larger Quality Learning Circle group reconvenes to share what they have learned during their study of a particular theme. It may be that certain examples of effective practice incur particular mention and are then shared with the wider community through a full faculty meeting. Following this initial experience, the group could initiate discussions on the next theme.

In summary, Quality Learning Circles include the following:

- heterogeneous groups of teachers drawn from different career stages, grades, and specialist groups;
- stable membership of five or six teachers engaged in a year's developmental work together;
- each group being joined by the principal for a few meetings;
- a three-step sequence of discussion, storytelling, reflection, and analysis within the group; observation in classrooms to enhance the meaning of the stories where the visitor to the classroom is the *learner*; and discussion of observations in pairs and then with the whole group;
- sharing examples of effective practice with the whole staff;
- following a set of themes throughout the year.

Thematic Supervision

In-class supervision has been criticized for its emphasis on teachers' professional shortcomings, and for the way it isolates teachers from the support and example of colleagues. Quality Learning Circles are one example of a departure from the problem- and individual-centered approach to in-class supervision. They rest on the assumption that teaching can and should be a collaborative rather than a solitary activity, and that there is more to be gained by considering a common theme within a group of colleagues than by focusing exclusively on one's individual professional shortcomings with a single supervisor. There are other methods and initiatives that also incorporate classroom observation and teacher/teacher or teacher/administrator collaboration, such as The Learning Network (see Appendix B).

The practical issue becomes one of selecting the common discussion theme for the Quality Learning Circles. Should it be a matter of democratic choice where individual members suggest themes for group consensus? This would certainly be a possibility, though it may be asking a lot from a newly formed group. The authors suggest an alternative.

Teachers in a school are faced with similar challenges to one another, and have much to learn from each other about meeting these challenges. Many challenges follow an annual, developmental cycle in the life of the school, and this cycle suggests a sequence of supervision activities for the whole school. A summary of this annual cycle might include the following stages from the beginning of the school year:

- establishing classroom routines and a base level of order permitting teaching and learning to take place;
- developing an appropriate classroom culture

Teachers in a school are faced with similar challenges to one another.

that establishes norms for group work, individual rights, learning, and any other important
values;
• identifying, monitoring, and recording learning outcomes and how these are reported to
parents and others;
• refocusing attention on curriculum and teaching and learning goals for the remainder of the
year.

This sequence of issues corresponds broadly
to the sequence of developmental issues most
teachers face through a school year and provides
a basis for a series of classroom observation visits. It is not essential that the sequence be followed as outlined. Indeed, to be effective it should
be adapted to the needs of each particular faculty. Faculties may choose to implement their
own specific sequence for a particular purpose, or
for a particular time.

There are a number of advantages of adopting a thematic approach to supervision rather
than persevering with the problem-centered clinical supervision procedures:

• teacher anxiety is reduced–Thematic Supervision places the focus on a series of developmental tasks in the annual cycle of the classroom,
and not on the problems or difficulties teachers
may be having;
• the process is one that encourages collaboration across the whole school–the progress
made by individual teachers will vary, but at
any point in the year all the staff will be working on the same basic theme;
• the process will emphasize attainable short-
term goals rather than presenting teachers
with impossibly ambitious targets for self-im-
provement–teachers only have so much energy
available for teacher development activities,
and they are likely to become more committed
to a program that can deliver realistic, but lim-

ited goals than one that promises much, but delivers little;

- the observing teacher will be the learner rather than the supervisor–each theme should provide teachers with the opportunity to share some aspect of their classroom practice with a colleague, with the visitor there to observe and learn from the work of a colleague, not to criticize and propose alternative practices;

- teachers will get frequent, positive, and supportive feedback–in general, teachers will be displaying aspects of their teaching practice in which they feel they have achieved something worthwhile, and not constantly exposing their shortcomings;

- the focus of discussion and observation will increase in complexity as the year progresses–as teachers become more familiar with each other's practice, and as their powers of reflection and group sharing become more practiced, they are likely to become more ambitious in the issues they research and develop;

- a thematic approach will require teachers to use a variety of data-gathering instruments–teachers will be less likely to become stuck in a limited and habitual response to classroom challenges;

- each year will follow a similar sequence–teachers will recognize that progress made in one year can be picked up and pursued in subsequent years through an annual, cyclical process, allowing new staff to enter at any point and not feel they have missed out irrevocably on some earlier stages;

- the annual cycle may be the same each year, but there is scope for emphases to change as the faculty becomes more confident in the process–as faculty members resolve many of the issues associated with establishing classroom routines and developing a supportive learning culture, they can spend more time in later years considering issues about learning outcomes and meeting students' individual needs.

Some examples of other possible themes may show how Quality Learning Circles and Thematic Supervision might work within just one theme.

Theme: Classroom Routines

The first theme for the year will normally relate to custodial care and promoting effective classroom routines. Across the school this will be the dominant theme for each Quality Learning Circle as teachers spend time observing each other, reflecting on their own observed practice and what they were trying to do, and how effective their various approaches are. Members of each Quality Learning Circle, following their observations of each other, would discuss the following types of questions:

- Were organizational routines clearly in place?
- Did all students know what was expected of them?
- Are classroom relationships becoming warm and respectful?
- Were all students actively engaged in learning when they were expected to be?
- Were appropriate teaching and learning resources readily available?

When each Quality Learning Circle has completed a cycle of classroom observation and discussion, it is worthwhile to have the whole faculty together to reflect on the theme. The group discussions will have identified some examples of particularly effective classroom practices that could be shared more widely. The exercise can be expanded beyond the classroom, and teachers can be encouraged to gather data and ask analytic questions related to school-wide routines such as bus arrival, recess, dismissal, and movement in the hallways. When teachers have worked on and are comfortable with the established routines in their classrooms and school-wide, the Quality Learning Circle theme can move to the development of classroom culture, and so on through the sequence.

The important and different aspect of Thematic Supervision is that the whole faculty focuses on the selected theme at the same time, and that information from this exercise is shared with colleagues through the Quality Learning Circles. Teachers are not asked to reveal their professional problems or shortcomings unless they wish to. In this way the traditionally isolated activity of teaching becomes a school-wide, collaborative effort. There is still room within the data gathering and feedback for teachers to talk with colleagues whom they trust about problems they wish to share and ideas they wish to evaluate. The priority, however, is to positively reinforce teachers for what they are already doing and to establish a culture throughout the school that encourages them to take some risks by shifting their practice toward greater effectiveness.

Each of the other themes has just as many possibilities for inquiry, though they are certainly not closely defined and circumscribed recipes for successful practice. A few more examples may indicate the range of questions and data gathering that could take place.

Teachers are not asked to reveal their professional problems or shortcomings unless they wish to.

Theme: Classroom Culture

Some suggested questions pertaining to classroom culture are:

- To what extent is student participation spontaneous?
- To what extent do individuals interact?
- What percentage of the teacher's time is spent

on control as opposed to engaging students in learning?
- Does the teacher group and regroup according to needs?
- How are individual learning needs met?
- Do students cooperate well?
- Is there an obvious enjoyment of learning?
- How are disputes and misunderstandings managed?

Theme: Learning Outcomes

Some suggested questions regarding learning outcomes are:

- What assessment samples of new learning are used?
- Is new learning evaluated in terms of the students' next learning steps?
- Is planning for new learning based on those learning needs?
- Are the instructional approaches appropriate to the learning needs?
- How is new learning reinforced?
- What forms of reinforcement are used?
- How is students' learning progress to be reported?

Theme: Curriculum and the Instructional Program

Some suggested questions about curriculum and the instructional program are:

- To what extent is the instructional program consistent with the state or district frameworks?
- How are study topics selected?
- What is the relationship between reading and writing in the classroom program?

- To what extent are teaching and learning objectives achieved?
- How does the teacher know this?
- To what extent do students schedule and plan their day?
- To what extent do students learn from each other?
- Are teaching and learning resources matched to the needs of the students?
- Is the teaching approach matched to the resource?

Focus on Skillful Teaching

To summarize, Thematic Supervision working within the Quality Learning Circle framework can replace the practice of in-class supervision. It retains many essential features of in-class supervision, that is, it is cyclical; it is collaborative; it focuses on patterns of teaching and learning behavior; and it is subject to professional ethical controls.

However, it avoids many drawbacks of in-class supervision. The process no longer focuses on the problems that teachers are assumed to be having. Classroom observation follows a cycle of themes that match the development of classroom life through the school year. Teachers share their observations and experiences with a group of colleagues who can afford to operate in a supportive and noncritical way together. They visit each others' classrooms as learners rather than as supervisors, identifying and reinforcing good practice where they find it. And through the discussions and reflections of the Quality Learning Circles they get an opportunity to clarify and add meaning to what they have observed.

Many professional development initiatives incorporate classroom observation followed by indepth inquiry and discussion among teachers and administrators. The terminology used in them may differ slightly from that used in the Quality Learning Circle framework. They may speak of teacher leaders, observation, instructional dialogue, or a critical triangle made up of teachers, outside consultants, and administrators, but the intent is the same. The emphasis should always remain on skillful teaching and good classroom practice.

Part IV

Appraisal

Part IV

Appraisal

The two chapters in this section turn attention to quadrants III and IV of the developmental matrix and the issue of appraisal. The focus of the next chapter is on principal appraisal, with discussion about school appraisal. Through the leadership of an effective principal should also emerge the attributes of an effective school. The authors have also noted that an effective school is one that results from the capacity of its teachers to meet the learning needs of the students as part of their mutual responsibility within the school community. The extent to which a school can do that, and the professional development needs of principals and teachers, is one of the purposes of appraisal explored in Chapters 8 and 9.

Chapter 8

Appraising the Principal

Describing the Principal's Job

Principals lead complex organizations. They are responsible for their own organizations, yet accountable to a board that represents the interests of those who have "invested" (in the case of school boards, parents and taxpayers) in the services the board provides. In the administration of schools, principals are usually not directly accountable to the board, but work through the local superintendent of schools. The school board is concerned more with the development of broad policy than the day-to-day operation of schools. The board relies on the superintendent and the principals for most aspects of school management. Through the superintendent, a principal has an important responsibility for carrying out the school board's policy through the leadership decisions he or she makes across every aspect of the life and work of the school. To do this effectively, the principal needs to be clear about the board's policies and policy priorities, and know how well he or she is performing as a school leader in accomplishing the requirements of these priorities. Whether formally or not, in most

A principal has an important responsibility for carrying out the school board's policy through the leadership decisions he or she makes across every aspect of the life and work of the school.

197

school districts principals are appraised on their performance at regular intervals. This appraisal will almost certainly be a superintendent's responsibility. The appraisal process takes many forms. It may be based on the school's performance within a regular regime of standardized testing. It can be a formal presentation of a report to a school board meeting. Or, it can be a periodic interview with the superintendent where there are varying degrees of structure and formality.

Ad hoc arrangements for appraising a principal's performance can be fraught with difficulties. They leave both the appraised and appraiser vulnerable, and if things go wrong, very often unfairly penalized. Like chief executives of most organizations, principals are called upon to demonstrate increased accountability, in their case for both educational performance and the expenditure of the taxpayer's money. Like chief executives in both for-profit and more especially not-for-profit organizations, some formal process for accountability can benefit both partners in the process. Issues related to appraising job performance are never easy to resolve, but many common tangles can be avoided when the process is clearly understood by all of the parties involved.

The following three essential components are needed to develop an effective principal appraisal process. A principal should have:

- a formal job description clearly stating the requirements of the position;
- an opportunity to negotiate performance objectives in key areas with the superintendent;
- a requirement to report regularly to the superintendent on his or her performance in each of these key areas.

While the appraisal process is conceptually straightforward, it can be a challenging task for most principals and district superintendents. Principals will feel vulnerable if they are not fully involved in negotiating every aspect of the appraisal process. They will be understandably wary of any appraisal system that is poorly defined and that could allow special interest groups or issues to take the appraisal in unexpected directions. There is always the temptation to seek an agreement that highlights those aspects of the principal's job that are most clearly defined and least problematic, such as staff and resource management. These are areas where performance indicators are easy to specify and relatively easy to measure. School boards, on the other hand, will seek an appraisal system that provides a regular and formal accounting for the performance of the principal and for the direction and progress of the whole school. A conscientious board will not be content with indications that the principal is doing the right kind of things. Boards want reassurance that what the principal does as a school leader results in improved student performance, and that there is evidence to prove it. This means that an appraisal of the principal's performance must also be an appraisal or review of what is happening across the whole school.

This interpretation of the appraisal process has some important implications for the principal's job description. In fairness, a principal should only be appraised on what is covered in the job description. The traditional approach of listing all the principal's many tasks and responsibilities in the job description provides little guidance to either the principal or the superintendent. A lengthy list of duties is seldom an indicator of the district's priorities or whether the implicit objectives in such a list are consistent with the board's long-term goals. A list of duties provides a superintendent or school board with little more than a checklist of administrative duties and no way of appraising the principal's performance against any of them. Using such a list as the basis for appraisal leaves room for several outcomes. The most likely action is that the superintendent will report on those task aspects of the principal's job highlighted in the document. Again, these are likely to be the organizational aspects of the school and the managerial and resource responsibilities that tend to be the most time-consuming for boards and their superintendents, yet seldom have a direct influence on a principal's overall performance as a school leader. Organizational matters are those kinds of responsibilities most superintendents would already be well informed about anyway. Another outcome is that principals who report on the organizational aspects of the school are reporting on a wide range of tasks and activities that have only an indirect bearing on the primary purpose of the school, which is teaching and learning. A report that dwells on organizational matters is usually only concerned with inputs–those things such as funding, staffing, and facilities–as measures of performance, not the impact these resources have on learning outcomes. Inevitably, such a report would be somewhat superficial. Important issues about student learning and about the school performing as an organization primarily concerned with teaching and learning are unlikely to be addressed.

A Framework for Appraisal

A very different approach to principal appraisal is being proposed in this chapter. David Stewart and Tom Prebble have developed a broad conceptual framework for a system of principal appraisal as part of their work with principals and schools in New Zealand. Their approach to the appraisal is consistent with the requirements of fully site-based managed schools in that coun-

try where, in 1989, the educational district structure was disestablished and each school granted
its own school board (Stewart and Prebble 1993).

Stewart and Prebble's concept of principal
appraisal is based on an assumption that both
the principal and the school board view the
appraisal process as an opportunity to examine
the central aspects of the school's mission and
performance as a measure of the principal's leadership. They argue that the process of appraisal
needs to begin with a very different kind of job
description for the principal—one that focuses on
the core activities of teaching and learning and
the support the principal provides to ensure that
the school is achieving its objectives in terms of
student growth and development. Rather than a
list of diverse tasks and responsibilities, the job
description should place the principal's attention
and efforts on the central mission of the school
and the contribution required to carry out that
mission. It can be a relatively short document,
and one that could apply equally well to the principal of any school committed to establishing the
kind of collaborative learning community this
book is about.

The job description should place the principal's attention and efforts on the central mission of the school and the contribution required to carry out that mission.

Themes

Stewart and Prebble's work with principals
suggests that there are at least five important
themes in educational and professional leadership:

- leading, coordinating, and facilitating a learning community;
- managing and developing a school culture;
- being responsible for a school's communication
  networks;
- playing a figurehead role in representing the
  school;

The key objective for the principal should be to provide leadership, direction, and vision for a developing learning community.

- maintaining a program of personal professional development.

Leading, Coordinating, and Facilitating the Learning Community

It is essential to the development of an effective school that the first priority of a principal should be to encourage learning. The concept of instructional leadership, which was promoted during the 1980s, helped redirect principals' attention from an exclusive concern for business and staff management to what was happening inside the classrooms. While this remains an important focus, it is necessary to broaden this perspective to involve the whole school community in the process of learning. It is only when *all* members of the school community focus on being learners that there can be the highest expectations for student learning. Schools change from being organizations that dispense knowledge and skills to communities where the process of learning is the most valued activity. Success in learning is then defined as individuals and groups constructing new meaning about the world.

The key objective for the principal should be to provide leadership, direction, and vision for a developing learning community. It is also important to manage the day-to-day affairs of the school, but these managerial activities should be seen as expressions of this leadership role rather than as ends in themselves. It is more important that the principal be able to think about teaching, to reflect about the pedagogy and classroom practice, and to promote a vision of how teaching and learning can develop more effectively in the school community.

An operating infrastructure has to be in place and working smoothly for reflection, debate, and inquiry to take place in a school community. Office systems, procedures for dealing with crises, and daily and weekly routine events have to function efficiently and within the cultural framework of the school. That is to say norms of behavior are established, rituals and taboos are adhered to, rites are recognized and celebrated, and events and relationships form a web of consistent and confirming interactions. The administrative and managerial responsibilities created by this infrastructure are not why schools exist. They are only support for the teaching and learning programs. The supervision of these activities lies clearly within the principal's responsibility, but should consume only a small proportion of time and energy. It is equally important that the staff who shares the management tasks of the school are just as strongly committed to the core culture of the school as the principal and faculty.

Managing and Developing the School Culture

Leadership skills are important but not sufficient qualities for the effective principal. It is also necessary to balance these skills with purpose, vision, and a commitment to what the school can become. People act and interpret the actions of others based on preconceptions, values, and beliefs. Within any organization or community, members are likely to share many of these assumptions and beliefs. These shared values are the roots of culture. Inevitably, leadership acts will be interpreted in terms of prevailing cultural beliefs and practices. Actions consistent with dominant cultural positions will be supported, while actions appearing to run counter to accepted practice and belief will be resisted. But culture is seldom static, nor is it likely to be universally shared or valued within a school community. People bring all manner of beliefs and expectations to their work within the school, and their behavior is likely to be deeply influenced by those attitudes and beliefs. A key role of leadership is to build unity and cohesion within the school com-

A key role of leadership is to build unity and cohesion within the school community by identifying a core set of beliefs and practices that support the direction in which the school should be developing.

munity by identifying a core set of beliefs and practices that support the direction in which the school should be developing, and then to take every opportunity to promote those core values and to socialize organizational members in those values.

The importance of shared cultural values extends right into the classrooms. Teachers' actions within their classrooms arise out of their beliefs about learning, about the value of the curriculum, and about the backgrounds and potential of the students. If principals wish to change what teachers do they must first change the way teachers think about what they do. The concept of culture provides a powerful mechanism for this work. Changing the culture of a school will not be an easy task. Unless the principal is able to do so, however, it is highly unlikely that any significant progress will be made in transforming the school into a learning community. A school where all the members can articulate the main aspects of their culture, and where they are passionately committed to the core beliefs of this culture, will be characterized by drive and influence in learning and teaching. A strong core culture is the hub of an effective school.

Taking Responsibility for School Communication Networks

If the goal is to create a learning community, and the strategy is to achieve this through the management of the school culture, then the careful management of communication networks within the school will be a key tactic in this process. A responsibility for communications is too broad a focus, so principals will need to concentrate on the communication networks that most critically affect the stability of school culture and the enhancement of the learning environment. There are two boundaries, or intersections, within the life of the school where the principal needs to take particular care in managing the flow of communications. The first is where the school and community intersect. The principal has the challenging task of promoting the school as a learning community to its parent community and beyond. This is a role the principal is uniquely placed to perform, and is not one that many principals can afford to delegate.

The second important intersection is between the core culture and the day-to-day affairs of the school. All communications within the school will be influenced by the core culture and the principal's task is to act both as a facilitator and as an interpreter. Members of the school community should be encouraged to relate all their plans, expectations, and perceptions to their understanding of the core culture. The principal needs to take a leading role in such discussions.

To know what is happening is essential to members in any enterprise, but in a school committed to working collaboratively, access to information provides the life blood of the community. All members of a school community must have access to up-to-date, relevant communication networks to function effectively. The principal is responsible for making this happen.

Playing a Figurehead Role in Representing the School

Until recently the role of figurehead was seen as the antithesis of effective leadership. "Figurehead" was the dismissive term applied to someone who was leader in name only. This was an understandable interpretation in an era that defined leadership in terms of its constituent functions of planning, organizing, directing, coordinating, and so on. However, once it is accepted that the management and direction of school culture is one of the most important responsibilities of the principal, this figurehead role takes on an entirely new significance.

*In a very real
sense the
principal
personifies the
school, its
culture, and its
mission.*

In a very real sense the principal personifies the school, its culture, and its mission. In this respect the principal is like a figurehead: at the head of the institution, showing the way, leading by example, and always visible. Staying with the analogy, the principal is an important figurehead for teachers and students of the school, and in a unique position to demonstrate and reinforce the core values of the school culture. There will be many occasions to use this figurehead role to its maximum advantage—when the school is brought together for celebrations such as graduation, special events, or festivals, and other occasions such as faculty meetings and when the school hosts a visitor. A school has regular opportunities to celebrate aspects of its culture in a ritualistic way; but every day there will be numerous less formal opportunities for the principal to hold up an aspect of the school culture that needs to be recognized and affirmed. This is a function that the principal is, by definition, uniquely able to perform.

For the community, this figurehead role may be the only role they ever see the principal perform, and it is likely to convey a strong impression of the character and quality of the school itself. While schools interact with their communities at a variety of levels and in many different ways, it is generally the principal who communicates officially with the local news media, who confirms any important agreement or contract, and who represents the school on any occasion of symbolic importance. The figurehead role extends beyond the narrow bounds of the school organization and conveys an aura of wider authority on the school leadership. The principal will often be seen as a trusted community leader—someone who is knowledgeable about the school community and about educational and social matters in general.

Personal Professional Development

It may seem unusual to list ongoing personal professional development as part of the principal's job description. It is done to emphasize the critical importance of the principal as a source of professional guidance and direction in the life of the effective school. Teachers know how difficult it can be to introduce a new idea or innovation into a school. They may be able to introduce it into their classrooms or programs, but probably no further than this. Attempts to influence the structure or direction of a whole school are not likely to be successful when driven solely by a classroom teacher. The research literature on educational innovation is virtually unanimous in underlining the importance of the principal in effecting significant school-wide change. If this is the case, it becomes critically important that the principal is constantly reflecting on the state of the school and the direction it should be taking.

This kind of professional reflection cannot be sustained solely by the daily life of a school. It needs to be informed by a constant flow of new ideas and insights. Some of the most important changes may come from collegial innovations such as Quality Learning Circles, but others will arise from participation in professional associations, participation in training workshops and conferences, and through personal reading and study.

How many busy school principals find the time to keep up with their professional reading? It is probably one of the first things to be sacrificed in the daily pressure of running a school. If principals are to continue to give their professional development the time and priority it needs, then they need to be reminded that this should be done. What better way than including this theme in their written job descriptions, and then reinforcing it by requiring an annual report on their professional development?

A Conceptual Job Description for a Principal

David Stewart and Tom Prebble have translated five themes of educational and professional leadership into five *responsibilities* that are described below as a principal's conceptual job description. Under each responsibility they propose *key objectives* and the *results expected* when those objectives are realized.

Responsibility 1. Lead, Coordinate, and Facilitate the Learning Community

Concept: Establish and maintain a school where learning is a highly valued activity by all members of the school community.

Key Objectives	Results Expected
Ensure that learning is the central focus of the school	Teachers seek learning success for students
	Teachers continue to learn new skills, new approaches, and widen their curriculum knowledge
	Parents and the wider school community are involved in learning
Develop an appropriate school curriculum	Within the district curriculum framework, the learning needs of students are being met through effective classroom programs
Expand the capacity of the faculty to meet a diverse range of student needs	Teachers' understandings are expanding and their classroom practices are becoming increasingly more effective
Facilitate the faculty in working together	Teachers work collaboratively to improve the effectiveness of the school as a learning community

Responsibility 2. Manage and Develop the School Culture

Concept: Develop a school culture in which learning is paramount and all individuals are encouraged, respected, and challenged intellectually, physically, and socially.

Key Objectives	Results Expected
Develop a school culture in which students feel safe, relaxed, and committed to learning	A progression of school development themes will be the focus for faculty activity
Maintain a school where new learning is based on existing strengths, and praise and positive reinforcement predominate	All students and staff will experience success based on learning progress
Ensure that the school is an orderly place where equipment, resources, and facilities are well managed	All members of the school community will be involved in decision making and management
Recognize individual differences and encourage a variety of teaching and learning approaches	Teachers and students will be given opportunities to work in a variety of ways
Provide a procedure for resolving misunderstandings and disputes	Distractions to learning will be kept to a minimum and disputes resolved rapidly

Responsibility 3. Take Responsibility for School Communication Networks

Concept: Act as a facilitator, interpreter, and network manager to ensure that the communication system allows all members of the school community to know what is happening.

Key Objectives	Results Expected
Ensure that the communications network is effective and efficient	Information will be freely available to those who need it Communication channels will be open
Ensure that information is continually being exchanged among the school, home, and the community	There will be continual monitoring of the quality and quantity of information
Ensure that parents have access to the appropriate communication networks	Parents will know what is happening within the school and will have the opportunity to consult and be consulted
Ensure that the core culture of the school is reflected through all communication networks	The agreed beliefs, shared understandings, and norms of the school community are reflected in the life of the school

Responsibility 4. Play a Figurehead Role in Representing the School

Concept: Represent and act for the school as the educational leader.

Key Objectives	Results Expected
Be the identifiable leader of the school community	Members of the wider community will identify the principal with the school in a positive manner
Speak and act on behalf of the school	The principal will have the confidence of the teachers, students, parents, and the school board
Ensure that the core culture of the school is at the hub of school activities	Teachers and students will value activities that are consistent with the core values of the school
Bring to the school knowledge, ideas, and examples from other educational settings	New ideas and practices are critically evaluated
Vigorously promote the school as an effective institution	The distinctive values and achievements of the school will be widely acknowledged in the community

Responsibility 5. Principal's Professional Development

Concept: Maintain an understanding of developing trends in education, keeping up-to-date in school leadership and curriculum development and participating in principal development activities.

Key Objectives	Results Expected
Read a variety of educational articles and journals	Incorporate new ideas into leadership repertoire
Take part in principal and leadership development activities	Discuss, examine, and modify present leadership and management practices
Share ideas and practices with colleagues	Take advantage of faculty meetings and other occasions to promote new ideas and practices
Visit other schools and host visits from other educators	Develop a philosophy of School Development that reflects an openness to review
Take an active part in teacher development	Develop an active, reflective approach to improving professional competence

The Mesa Experience

The following case study describes what happened in the Mesa School District when it was required by state mandate to implement a system of principal appraisal.

The schools in Mesa School District–five elementary, one middle, and one high school–have a relatively homogeneous and stable student population. The school committee of the town board is keenly contested and its activities are always a focus of local discussion. The schools are well funded and maintained and provide an educational environment of good quality. It was in this context that the superintendent and the principals considered their task.

One of the authors, Peter Duncan, was invited to work with the Mesa principals. He introduced them to the broad conceptual framework for a system of principal appraisal developed by David Stewart and Tom Prebble. As a result, a "working statement" about the purpose of the appraisal system was a helpful first step for this group. After considerable discussion and debate the group stated: "Appraisal is concerned with the performance of a school where the principal is an effective educational and professional leader achieving an agreed set of school results consistent with the district's broad educational priorities." This statement remained open to review.

Note that this statement views appraisal as the performance of the school as an organization, not simply the principal's performance in a range of duties. The effectiveness of the school reflects a principal's leadership across a range of areas. The Mesa principals expanded this notion by developing their own guidelines for the district system:

- principal appraisal should seek to improve the quality of educational achievement in the Mesa School District through supporting teachers in meeting the educational needs of every student in the school system;
- the performance of the school toward achieving the district's priorities should be seen as a reflection of the principal's leadership in certain key areas of performance;
- school and principal appraisal should serve the function of informing the community about the quality of their investment in education.

They also discussed three other key attributes that an effective appraisal system needs to accomplish:

Note that this statement views appraisal as the performance of the school as an organization, not simply the principal's performance in a range of duties.

- The appraisal should achieve its stated purpose of providing relevant information about educational performance. At the end of the appraisal period the principal should know to what extent his or her school leadership resulted in progress toward the district achieving its educational priorities. The principals would together discuss these priorities at the beginning of the appraisal period. Each building principal would then seek agreement with the superintendent about the school objectives relevant to those priorities and the quality of evidence that would support their accomplishment.

- It must be fair to each of the interested parties. On the one hand the community's investment in the school system is accounted for by the efficient and effective management of the school and the timely and meaningful reporting to parents about their children's educational progress. On the other hand, the principal's performance expectations should be clearly stated in the agreement with the superintendent. These performance results should be those that superintendent and principal agree could reasonably be achieved during the appraisal period.

- Appraisal must provide a foundation for further development of both the principal and the school.

The existing strengths of people and schools should be further developed as part of the appraisal procedure, rather than allow it to focus on weaknesses. The process should be viewed as a new starting point for the personal and professional development of the principal, as well as for the organizational development of the school. Appraisal becomes a continuing process; a periodic review of the school as it moves toward the achievement of clear and purposeful teaching and learning goals.

The conventional way that the Mesa School District committee gained a sense of what was happening in schools came from principals' annual reports presented by the superintendent. Other than occasional, usually formal, visits to a school, the annual report was the only information available to the committee. That reporting process provided little guidance about those aspects of school leadership that had any impact on student achievement.

Implementing the Mesa Principal Appraisal Scheme

Before discussing the proposed Mesa School District's appraisal system in any detail, it may be helpful to consider the procedure that was agreed upon for implementing the system. The following sequence was proposed:

- principals and the superintendent would consider the broad district priorities for the appraisal period;
- together they would discuss the results common to all schools that in the long run could be expected by working toward these priorities;
- each building principal in a separate conference with the superintendent would consider how the district's expected results might be achieved by establishing a set of school-specific objectives. They would also agree on what dates through the year progress would be formally reviewed and what indicators would be used to assess progress toward the results;
- at the conclusion of the appraisal period each principal would report to the superintendent on each school's achievements, and the superintendent, in turn, would report on the district's achievements to the board.

The sequence of steps for implementing the scheme was a turning point at which each principal realized the impact of the proposal on their school leadership.

The development of the sequence for this procedure was an important phase in the establishment of the appraisal system. Up to this point the issues could be considered, discussed, and agreed upon, but without any real commitment to action. The sequence of steps for implementing the scheme was a turning point at which each principal realized the impact of the proposal on their school leadership. Some new issues emerged. For example, it was noted that too often during the year there are things beyond a building principal's control that would make it impossible to achieve what could seem like a perfectly reasonable objective at the beginning of the year. This raised a question about the extent to which site objectives were open to review. It was proposed that a number of review dates throughout the appraisal period left room for both principals and the superintendent to discuss progress. At the same time, there would be an opportunity to reconsider, and if necessary amend, the school's objectives according to any special circumstances. This meant that changes could be accomplished in a managed, responsible way. This review provision did not offer an escape hatch for lax leadership, and there would need to be clear evidence as to why any school objective was considered for amendment.

The Mesa Appraisal System as It Evolved

The discussion and debate prompted by the Stewart and Prebble framework developed a system of appraisal that began to meet the particular needs of the Mesa School District. To conform to the state's requirements for administrative standards, the principal's responsibilities proposed in the Stewart and Prebble framework were translated into *standards* and the final drafts began to reflect this requirement. Six standards consistent with the district's priorities were proposed, each with a set of *expected results*. Under the expected results each principal, in consultation with the superintendent, developed a further set of school *objectives* for the appraisal period as set out below as one of the district's drafts.

The Mesa School District Draft of Administrative Standards for Principals

Standard One

Recognize that learning is a continuum and that administration and faculty must develop a consistent set of understandings and practices that support a common view of student progress and achievement.

Results Expected

The principal

- observes, evaluates, and provides specific feedback regarding staff performance to ensure high levels of professional standards;
- assists and supports teachers in gaining the new understandings needed to make changes in practice that supports student learning and achievement;
- provides opportunities and resources for all staff to engage in professional development that enhances faculty understanding and results in increased learning and development for a diverse student population.

School Objectives

(To be completed by each principal in consultation with the superintendent.)

Standard Two

Support the staff in analyzing and planning units, courses, and programs so that instructional time engages students and focuses on essential skills, concepts, and understandings.

Results Expected

The principal

- assists teachers in the development of inquiry-based practices that link authentic assessment and learning;
- involves the faculty in curriculum planning and program development that is relevant to students and their pursuit of life-long learning;
- monitors the implementation of the district's curriculum throughout the school.

School Objectives

(To be completed by each principal in consultation with the superintendent.)

Standard Three

Coordinate and facilitate a learning community that engages students, teachers, parents, and the community to improve learning outcomes (involve students, teachers, parents, and the community in the learning process).

Results Expected

The principal

- builds unity and cohesion by developing and encouraging consistent, high-quality teaching and learning practices;

- emphasizes student learning as the focus of all school programs and activities;
- promotes an environment and culture where learning, creativity, the exchange of ideas, responsible risk-taking, and experimentation are seen as shared, practical, and valuable;
- designs opportunities for, and involves others in, inquiry resulting in setting, monitoring, and accomplishing goals based on the needs of the school community;
- develops, participates in, and maintains systems of shared decision making with school colleagues and the larger school community.

School Objectives

(To be completed by each principal in consultation with the superintendent.)

Standard Four

Establish and manage communication networks within the school and among the school, parents, and the community.

Results Expected

The principal

- communicates the school vision, goals, needs, and accomplishments clearly and concisely using reliable data, information, and analysis;
- provides information to parents and community members through handouts, brochures, news articles, informational sheets, public meetings, demonstrations, and the like;
- establishes a range of formal and informal communication channels that are open to two-way information flows.

School Objectives

(To be completed by each principal in consultation with the superintendent.)

Standard Five

Provide management that functions effectively as a support for the school's focus on teaching and learning.

Results Expected

The principal

- uses an ongoing process to assess, review, and evaluate when making decisions regarding resource allocations, facilities, and equipment management to ensure congruence with school goals and objectives;
- ensures that the school is an orderly place where facilities, equipment, and resources are well managed and processes are well defined;
- involves others in financial planning activities such as analyzing and evaluating resources to meet building plan goals and translating program needs into cost requirements;
- understands, interprets, and upholds applicable laws, regulations, policies, and procedures.

School Objectives

(To be completed by each principal in consultation with the superintendent.)

Standard Six

Demonstrate the importance of professional development in the life-long learning process.

Results Expected

The principal

- questions current practices and continuously pursues open dialogue and reflection to find new ways to solve problems;
- develops and implements a professional development plan which focuses specific action toward ongoing professional development.

Personal Objectives

(To be completed by the principal in consultation with the superintendent.)

The Standards in Action

The following is one example of how a principal established a set of building objectives. Nancy is the principal of a kindergarten to grade five elementary school in the Mesa School District. Her school has a good record of collaborative decision making. Over the past school year she has kept the faculty's focus on developing students as competent readers. Nancy understands that teachers will only meet the learning needs of their students in reading development if they have a range of assessment data that informs them about reading progress. A few of her teachers had been introduced to running records, a procedure that enables the teacher to assess progress in reading by recording aspects of students' reading behavior as they are reading to the teacher. Both Nancy and a growing number of her faculty had agreed on the value of running records as an assessment tool. A next step would be to demonstrate their usefulness as an assessment tool and to encourage all teachers to use them. Following discussions with the faculty and superintendent she proposed a school objective for Standard Three that stated: *"By the end of this school year all teachers will use running records as a reading assessment tool."*

Nancy was aware that in learning to use running records, teachers would be learning more about the reading process, which in turn would point to the crucial importance of students being read to daily through the grades. To this she linked the responsibility that parents should be taking in supporting the school reading program. In turn, the school could encourage this responsibility by opening up the library as a source of books for parents to read aloud to their children. The faculty had also discussed an extended role that parents might play in planning for this initiative and operating the school library. With this in mind the second school objective stated that the school would: *"Develop the role of the school library by actively involving parents in its work and improving their access to its resources."*

These examples suggest that the scope of the school objectives are limited to small steps on the way to meeting the expected results. These results, in the long run, reflect both the priorities of the school committee (indeed, the process assists to clarify them) who represent the broader community and the leadership responsibilities of the principal. Appraisal of a principal need not be, and indeed should not be, threatening or potentially punitive. In these examples Nancy has the opportunity to develop her faculty, her school, and herself as a school leader. Working with her superintendent, and using the skills of her leadership, there is little reason why she and the faculty should not be successful in meeting all the objectives they establish as part of the appraisal process.

The approach to appraisal that is proposed in the Mesa example is in marked contrast to more conventional methods of appraising the principal. Increasingly, principals are required to report their progress in achieving specifically listed performance targets. Experience with this particular import from the commercial world is fairly limited. It is of doubtful effectiveness in a school setting because there are countless human and other variables over which a principal has little or no control. More importantly, performance of their managerial tasks can only have limited and indirect bearing on the learning experience that tasks place within classrooms. In contrast, the approach presented here suggests that the principal appraisal process is an opportunity for the school community to review the direction of the school in general and the effectiveness of the school leadership in particular. In a school committed to establishing a collaborative learning community it makes little sense to focus exclusively on the role and activities of the principal when assessing the effectiveness of the school's leadership. That effectiveness can only finally be determined by looking at the key goals and objectives that are being pursued by the school leadership and determining how well they are being achieved in terms of their impact on the school. Principal appraisal becomes an acceptable and necessary form of a continuing school review.

Teachers and parents need to be involved in the appraisal and review processes if they are to be drawn into the learning community. The review process becomes an important school development activity while still fulfilling the appraisal requirements. This wider school and community involvement can come with a cost. It takes time and effort to involve the community in the appraisal process, to conduct surveys of parents and students, to feed the data back, and to study their significance. It is not practical to attempt a review (or appraisal) of every aspect of school leadership and goal achievement each

The principal appraisal process is an opportunity for the school community to review the direction of the school in general and the effectiveness of the school leadership in particular.

year. If the school community is to be asked to commit itself wholeheartedly to this process, it is probably unrealistic to expect a superintendent to complete a thorough review of more than one set of the principal's leadership objectives in each cycle. For instance, the principal and superintendent could agree to study the leadership and development of the learning community one year. In the next year, the focus could be on student achievement, the effectiveness of curriculum programs, and the impact of innovations such as Quality Learning Circles or The Learning Network that are part of the participant's personal and professional development. The following year the theme might be the management and development of the school culture, when the superintendent would be seeking information on the development of safe, committed classroom environments, the use of preferred styles of behavior management, the commitment to principles of equity in the daily life of the school, and so on.

A review committed to this alternative approach to principal appraisal, and a school community prepared to invest the energy to make it work, means this aspect of school life becomes an important means for developing school culture. It is not an easy option, but it is a rewarding one. There is a commitment to gathering data and organizing and encouraging wider involvement in the process by teachers, students, and parents. There is also a need to shoulder responsibilities for shortcomings that are uncovered as well as being encouraged by the successes. The focus for the principal has to be wider than the administrative and desk work that tends to dominate most conventional efforts at principal appraisal. Instead, leadership responsibilities become those associated with important aspects in the work, including the:

• teaching and learning that takes places in each

classroom;

- establishment of a supportive, learning-based school culture;
- way the school communicates and maintains its links with the wider community;
- direction the school is taking and the way that this direction is portrayed;
- processes of constant review and revitalization of the school and its programs.

Unlike office work and financial management, these are issues that resist managerial control. At best a principal and teachers will be able to report steady progress in each of these areas; they will not be reporting a perfect performance. These areas of appraisal are also areas that are value-laden and controversial. Few people will quibble over a building maintenance schedule, but issues of school culture are more problematic. The work of School Development is gradual and deliberate. As with other organizational improvement approaches, School Development is not a one-shot, quick-fix solution. It is a style of leadership that will yield its results over the medium and longer term and require sustained effort and commitment by the whole school. The approach the authors have suggested for principal appraisal is a means of consistently reviewing that progress.

School Development is not a one-shot, quick-fix solution. It is a style of leadership that will yield its results over the medium and longer term.

Chapter 9

Teacher Appraisal

Describing the Teacher's Job

The teacher's task is to create a classroom culture that supports, encourages, and facilitates active learning. This is a culture where students build on their prior understandings and work with others to construct new views of the world for themselves. Creating stimulating and challenging environments for young people requires routines and shared understandings about how decisions should be made, how conflict will be resolved, and how achievement will be recognized. These microcultures are dynamic but fragile and need to be planned and monitored carefully.

If principals hope to influence what teachers are doing they must first encourage them to reflect on what they are doing. A teacher's job description is an important starting point in this process. In the previous chapter the authors discussed the drawbacks of a typical principal's job description as a statement listing a series of tasks and responsibilities. For teachers, the same kind of tasks and responsibilities document may be useful in an organization made up of interlocking specialized roles and where the formal job descriptions clearly state what each person does and how their work relates to that of their col-

The teacher's task is to create a classroom culture that supports, encourages, and facilitates active learning.

227

This approach to teacher appraisal concentrates on what teachers are trying to achieve in their work rather than identifying a series of discrete tasks in which they engage.

leagues. In a complex and multifaceted job such as teaching, a formal job description is seldom very helpful, either for guiding the teacher's classroom practice or to a principal holding a teacher accountable for the students' learning that results from it. Too often written job descriptions give unwarranted emphasis to all the non-classroom responsibilities teachers carry, such as supervising an area of the curriculum or organizing special programs, while saying little that is helpful about classroom teaching and learning outcomes.

David Stewart and Tom Prebble have considered an alternative approach to the teachers' appraisal similar to that proposed for principals. It begins with the ideas, concepts, and intentions that teachers bring to their work and is developed into a Conceptual Job Description that broadly defines the work of all the teachers in a school. This approach to teacher appraisal concentrates on what teachers are trying to achieve in their work rather than identifying a series of discrete tasks in which they engage. As they did with the principal appraisal framework, Stewart and Prebble identify five themes used as a framework for a teacher job description that would apply to all teachers in a school:

- classroom teaching;
- classroom culture;
- personal professional development;
- school culture;
- specific responsibilities.

Classroom Teaching

The primary concern for any teacher must be *teaching and learning*–supporting students to acquire new knowledge and skills. A job description should draw attention to the following:

- assessing prior learning;
- evaluating that assessment in terms of what the students can do, need to learn next, and what the teacher will do about it;
- planning for that instruction;
- implementing an appropriate instructional approach;
- assessing what learning has taken place.

The statement in a common job description relating to classroom practice need be no more detailed except to indicate very briefly the kind of result that should be expected against each objective. If a teacher's objective is: "to use an appropriate range of assessment tools in monitoring student progress in reading and writing," it is expected that this will be achieved by using and further developing a range of teacher assessment skills. Nancy, a principal in the Mesa School District discussed in examples in the previous chapter, identified the potential of running records as an assessment tool as one of her school objectives. As a teacher objective this is directly related to classroom practice, and one that requires continual teacher development. Because this development requires the principal's support, there should be an opportunity for teachers and the principal to record any difficulties or contingencies that may prevent a teacher from meeting an objective.

Classroom Culture

Teaching takes place within a social context—in a classroom with a unique *culture* that either supports or detracts from the teacher's efforts to encourage individual learning. It is possible for a school community to identify the classroom cultures it wishes to foster and the results that can be expected from such a culture.

Personal Professional Development

Studying and upgrading professional skills is vital to all members of the learning community, and it should be possible to indicate some objectives for *personal professional development* toward which teachers should be striving. Teachers vary in their understandings, experience, and levels of developed classroom practices. Under this heading could go any specific teacher development initiatives that meet the particular professional needs of each teacher.

School Culture

Classrooms have a contribution to make to the greater *school culture*, and they are deeply influenced by the prevailing values and customs of the wider school. Teachers need to acknowledge their responsibility in building an appropriate school culture and communicating the central messages of that culture to their students, the parents, and the wider school community.

Specific Responsibilities

Finally, most teachers will have *specific responsibilities* that must be listed in their job descriptions and that generate their own objectives and statements of anticipated results.

A Conceptual Job Description for Teachers

David Stewart and Tom Prebble have set out the five themes as teacher responsibilities within a Conceptual Job Description. Associated with each responsibility are the key objectives and the expected results.

Responsibility 1. Classroom Teaching

Concept: Provide quality learning opportunities based on the school's curriculum plan and targeted to the learning needs of students.

Key Objectives	Results Expected
Gather assessment data	Observable student progress
Evaluate assessment data	There is an awareness of next instructional step
Select appropriate resources	An appropriate range of instructional resources is available
Select appropriate learning experiences	The range of instructional approaches is broadening
Gather further assessment data	Evidence of student learning is available

Responsibility 2. Classroom Culture

Concept: Develop a classroom culture where individuals are encouraged, respected, and challenged intellectually, physically, and socially.

Key Objectives	Results Expected
Develop classrooms where students feel safe, relaxed, and committed to learning	There is a progression from custodial care to students being engaged in learning throughout the year
Ensure that tasks are within the capabilities of students	All students will experience success in learning
Maintain a classroom where praise and positive reinforcement predominate	Students will reinforce each other
Ensure that the classroom is an attractive, orderly place where equipment and resources are well managed	The classroom is a stimulating, constantly changing place with everyone involved in its maintenance
Recognize individual differences and provide for a variety of learning experiences	All students are able to work effectively in a variety of experiences
Provide a procedure for resolving misunderstandings and disputes	Distractions to learning are kept to a minimum and disputes are resolved rapidly

Responsibility 3. Personal Professional Development

Concept: Maintain an understanding of developing trends in education, keep up-to-date in curriculum development, and participate fully in teacher development programs.

Key Objectives	Results Expected
Read a variety of educational articles and journals	Incorporate new ideas into the teaching repertoire
Take part in school-based and district inservice education	Discuss, examine, and modify present teaching practice
Share ideas and practices with colleagues	Take an active part in small group and faculty meetings
Be involved in visiting and being visited by colleagues in the classroom and in subsequent discussions	Follow a thematic school development approach throughout the school year
Take an active part in observing colleagues' classroom practice	Develop an active, reflective-practice mode of improving professional competence

Responsibility 4. School Culture

Concept: Maintain a professional stance both with the school and within the community to foster the highest quality teaching and learning.

Key Objectives	Results Expected
Participate in student activities outside the classroom	Students are fully committed to educational activities outside the classroom and beyond the school
Communicate with parents or caregivers regarding student progress	Maintain a six-week reporting cycle Attend meetings with parents and offer interviews
Support the school's image in the community	Respect individual confidentiality Resolve problems within the institution Promote students' positive attributes Welcome visitors
Participate in whole-of-school events	Demonstrate a commitment to a collegial relationship
Promote appropriate and desirable student behavior	Listen to a variety of points of view Be available for individual help and advice Model courteous behavior Act fairly

Responsibility 5. Specific Responsibilities

Concept: Demonstrate to others by example effective and higher order skills as a classroom teacher and share with the principal the responsibility for promoting and maintaining an optimum learning community.

Specific duties/responsibilities: (The following is an example of the specific responsibilities of an elementary school teacher with curriculum leadership responsibilities.)

Key Objectives	Results Expected
Provide support for a variety of classroom practices through regular class teaching	Other teachers will seek advice and support regarding their classroom practice
Demonstrate knowledge, understanding, and support for the school's development objectives	Be able to communicate with colleagues, students, and parents about the essential elements of school life
Take responsibility for managing and coordinating delegated school activities	Problem-solving strategies are applied and effective outcomes are achieved
Promote professional dialogue through active participation and commitment to teaching and learning theory	All teachers will participate in professional dialogue

Setting Teacher Objectives

No matter how clear and succinct a job description may be, it will only be useful if it is seen to influence what teachers are actually doing in their classrooms. One way of ensuring that this happens is for the job description to become a central document in both the *development* and the *appraisal* activities of the school. For instance, considering the concept of "classroom culture" from the teacher's job description, the key objectives contributing to this concept could be subjects for faculty professional discussion for many months. For example, how teachers

No matter how clear and succinct a job description may be, it will only be useful if it is seen to influence what teachers are actually doing in their classrooms.

ensure that all students are experiencing success despite their varying backgrounds and experiences at each grade level; how teachers develop and maintain a supportive classroom climate; the variety of approaches that teachers are able to bring to their instruction; and the ways in which teachers resolve disputes and maintain harmonious working relationships within their classrooms are all topics concerned with classroom culture. Personal and professional development should be one component of the job description; appraisal must remain the other.

Personal Objectives

The job description defines what a teacher is meant to be doing and achieving in the job. This is accomplished through an opportunity for each teacher to set the individual objectives they wish to achieve in their work over the coming year. The personal objectives should correspond to the generic statements of *responsibilities, key objectives,* and *results expected* listed in their Conceptual Job Descriptions. These personal objective statements would be discussed and negotiated with the principal or other administrator. They should be selective, focus on new understandings the teacher wishes to develop about his or her own classroom practice, and be achievable yet challenging. Figure 9.1 suggests that the development and appraisal document attached to the teacher's job description needs to be little more than a page of clearly stated objectives agreed to between the principal or administrator and the teacher concerned.

Appraising Teachers

Another component of an appraisal system is the process by which a principal or another administrator on the principal's behalf monitors and reports on that teacher's performance.

Please write your major objectives under each of these headings. There will be an opportunity to discuss and revise these, if necessary, at the first appraisal meeting of the year.

1. Classroom Teaching

2. Classroom Culture

3. Personal Professional Development

4. School Culture

5. Specific Responsibilities

Signed

_____   _____

Teacher   Date

_____   _____

Principal   Date

Figure 9.1: Objective Setting: Goals for 19__

Attempts to prescribe a standard method of teaching and then appraise performance against that standard are doomed to acrimonious failure.

Supervision, monitoring, and appraisal are difficult and challenging activities for any organizational leader. As professionals, teachers are required to exercise a high level of individual judgment in addressing the constant flow of problems and decisions they are required to deal with each day. Anticipating the full range of decisions any teacher will be called on to make is not possible, nor is it possible to predetermine appropriate or "correct" responses to all these decisions. This means that systems of supervision and appraisal must recognize and accommodate the complexity of the teaching task. Attempts to prescribe a standard method of teaching and then appraise performance against that standard are doomed to acrimonious failure. Similarly, attempts to appraise teaching performance solely against crude measures of student learning outcomes will be equally unsuccessful. Unless the appraiser can factor in the myriad input and process variables that contribute to these outcomes, such an approach will do little more than reward those teachers who are fortunate to be teaching classes of able, committed students and penalize those who struggle with more challenging groups of learners.

Faced with this perennial and intractable dilemma, school administrators are frequently tempted to accede to the claim by teachers for their professional autonomy and avoid any direct involvement in teacher appraisals. But this response is just as unacceptable. There is no question that the quality of instruction has a direct and important impact on student learning outcomes and that the quality of teachers' instructional performance varies widely within most schools. It is a primary responsibility of principals to appraise the faculty on the quality of teaching and learning for which they are responsible. They are equally responsible to support, guide, and develop their skills and to ensure that all members of the faculty achieve more than a minimum level of competence.

In an earlier chapter it was strongly argued that the best way for a principal to improve the quality of classroom teaching is to encourage a culture of reflective discourse among the faculty. It is also necessary to have a regular, formal appraisal of each member of the faculty. This is to meet the mandated requirements and a teacher's contractual obligations and to provide that individual with support, guidance, and feedback that is not possible through more collegial staff development processes.

The Professional Development Consultation

There are many options for teacher appraisal. The approach being advocated here is a simple, straightforward process the authors call Professional Development Consultation, or PDC. This is a cycle of meetings between the principal (or other administrator, although all references here are to the principal) and each member of the faculty over a year. These meetings are called "professional development consultations" because this term seems to preserve the positive, collegial, and nonthreatening elements of supervision that should be stressed.

The purposes of the meetings are to:

- provide the formal opportunity for each teacher to discuss and evaluate goals and performance on a regular basis;
- allow the principal to monitor and facilitate the goal setting and job performance of each teacher;
- uncover problems and contingencies in the patterns of work relationships operating among faculty;
- provide a formalized and legitimate opportunity for teachers to evaluate the working relationship they have with the principal.

There are limits, determined by the size of a faculty, as to how often a principal can observe in classrooms. Where other administrators share the appraisal there needs to be a clear and shared sense of purpose among the team. The appraisal should not be viewed as a single visit to a classroom but the culmination of a series of regular observation visits that have been built into the administrator's own daily schedule. The task has implications for an administrator's own appraisal, providing a direct connection between roles and responsibilities of administrators and those of teachers.

The PDC in Action

The PDC will follow a similar course in most schools. The first consultation would take place early in the school year. Teachers would report their progress in setting objectives under each major heading of the job description. Discussion would probably follow the order of the major headings as they are set out in the teachers' Conceptual Job Description:

- classroom teaching;
- classroom culture;
- personal professional development;
- school culture;
- specific responsibilities;
- personal objectives.

Particular attention would be paid to the major objectives the teacher had listed under each heading. There would be opportunities to discuss key concepts, the results expected, and any possible issues arising out of that year's particular class composition or other unique features. At the conclusion of each topic the wording of each objective could be refined as appropriate and new personal objectives considered. New time lines would be noted.

A discussion on classroom culture, for example, may have raised the issue of potentially disruptive student disputes. A personal objective in this section could include: *developing skills and practices to resolve classroom and schoolyard disputes* with a time frame for implementing new practices. Together, the teacher and the principal would discuss why the teacher is concerned about this issue, what action is planned, and how realistic the proposed time line is. The teacher might add to the personal objective: *to have a set of new practices in place by October 31.*

At this early PDC meeting, a teacher would also share with the principal goals for personal and professional development, including enrollment in professional education programs for credit, proposed conference attendance, and other, less formal activities. The aim of the meeting is to provide an open and frank discussion about the teacher's role in the school and what strengths the teacher is able to contribute to school-wide activities. This first PDC meeting would conclude with the signing of an agreed-upon document.

The second PDC of the year would be held about halfway through the school year, again focused on the job description and in particular the teacher's agreed-upon objectives. The teacher would report on progress, presenting evidence to support the conclusions reached, and the principal would have an opportunity to present a cumulative picture that has emerged from classroom observations.

The teacher would also get the opportunity to comment on the district's and principal's support and constraints that have directly affected the quality of classroom instruction. This is an important part of PDC discussion–the analysis and comment should not be all one way, and might be guided by the following questions:

• What aspects of school organization and policy make your job more difficult?

Time should be spent discussing the teacher's professional development program, plans for further professional study, aspirations, and possible changes to duties and school-wide responsibilities.

- What do I do that makes your job more difficult?
- What might I do to offer greater support to you in your job?

Time should be spent discussing the teacher's professional development program, plans for further professional study, aspirations, and possible changes to duties and school-wide responsibilities. Toward the conclusion of this discussion the teacher should be invited to confirm or revise the set of objectives for the remainder of the year in the light of progress over the previous period, new insights from professional development, and the principal's comments.

The third and final PDC would be held toward the end of the school year. It would have many of the elements of the second PDC. Again the teacher would have the opportunity to report an analysis of progress toward the agreed-upon objectives, and the principal would have an opportunity to respond. This conversation could be an opportunity for a full summary discussion on the performance and professional development of the teacher through the appraisal period. This discussion is also an opportunity for the teacher and principal to look more strategically into the future based on the strengths both teacher and principal agree have been developing. With that knowledge it could be more profitable for the teacher to state some personal preferences that might influence upcoming decisions concerning staffing, organization, policy formation, and the allocation of duties and responsibilities for the following year.

The PDC as a Mechanism for Growth

The PDC is designed primarily as a tool of teacher development and appraisal, to have a direct impact on what teachers do in their classrooms and how they are accountable for it. Equally, a strength of the PDC is the formal link it offers between individual members of the faculty and the school administration where communication about goals, professional needs, objectives, and concerns can flow in both directions.

A growing number of schools are using the PDC, or very similar arrangements, as the basis for teacher development, supervision, and appraisal. For the most part, administrators and teachers are finding it an attractive option. Principals and other administrators recognize the important discipline of regular, purposeful, and focused classroom observations and the impact this has on their own professional development. They find the PDC is a helpful mechanism for keeping in regular contact with the work of all major areas in the school and welcome the opportunity to offer support and guidance in a professionally acceptable manner to their colleagues. More particularly, because the PDC is a discussion that enables *critical reflection* to occur for both the principal and the participating teacher, both can perceive each other as learners. Teachers appreciate the benefit of keeping the principal fully informed of their personal insights and challenges and what impact these are having on their classroom practice. They find that regular meetings give them an opportunity to discuss programs of work that meet the overall goals of the school and at best effectively meet the needs and interests of their students. The ability to negotiate criteria on which their own classroom practice will be appraised means that the full range of the strengths teachers bring to the job has less chance of being overlooked or misjudged by a principal whom they feel might not fully understand or appreciate what they are doing.

There is, nonetheless, an important caveat. Some principals have introduced the PDC without a great deal of prior discussion with the faculty. Recalling the four phases of School Development, the introduction of PDCs is a Phase 3 activity, as it can be a major structural change. Where PDCs have been introduced without the benefits of the previous phases, the scope for misunderstanding and failure is considerable. If teachers are unconvinced of the benefits they are likely to gain from the PDC, or if they fear that the principal may use it as an instrument of unalloyed managerial control, they are likely to resist the imposition and be so guarded in their discussion with administrators that any benefit from the introduction of the PDC is lost. Similarly, if a principal does not fully understand the underlying assumptions of the PDC, nor appreciates the reciprocal nature of the PDC discussion, there exists the temptation to regard the innovation as a device to increase control *over* the faculty, rather than a way of working *with* it. The message should be clear. A faculty and its administration need to be comfortably working together before a PDC is introduced. Consistent with a theme of this book, a school must go through an exercise of understanding its existing way of doing things, gathering data, and collaboratively analyzing that data before a PDC should be contemplated. These two phases of the School Development process provide the opportunity for self-reflection and discussion before the structural change of a PDC is made.

Part V

The School Development
Process in Action

Part V

The School Development Process in Action

The underlying themes of this book are concerned with schools becoming learning communities, and how principals and teachers can develop themselves professionally and collegially toward this end through a process of reflective practice. To develop the connection between these important concepts and the work of schools, principals, and teachers, a number of discrete but interrelated approaches were introduced in the form of a matrix (see Matrix II on following page).

The first and overarching approach is called School Development. This process is a cycle of developmental phases usually involving the whole faculty, and often including part of the wider school community, that addresses a challenge facing the school. Working with the diverse interests of a school community requires a systematic, structured approach to encourage participants to remain committed to the process and to the decisions that emerge from it. The School Development process has four phases. These are:

	School	Individual
Development	*Quadrant 1* *Four Phases of School Development* • Data collection • Collaboration • Structural change • Focus on teaching and learning	*Quadrant 2* *Principals and teachers engaging in reflective thought through:* • Quality Learning Circles • Thematic Supervision • Professional development and support beyond the school
Appraisal	*Quadrant 3* *School Review and Principal Appraisal* • Conceptual Job Description for the principal • Regular appraisal of the principal • Thematic review of the school	*Quadrant 4* *Teacher Appraisal* • Conceptual Job Description for all teachers • Professional Development Consultation cycle

Matrix II: Structure of *The Reflective Principal*

- Phase 1: data gathering–understanding current practices;
- Phase 2: collaborative analysis;
- Phase 3: structural change;
- Phase 4: a focus on teaching and learning.

It is necessary to take time to work through each phase in the cycle. Because of the complexities of school change, the time should be spent identifying the issues or problems, then gathering data to get a feel for their dimensions, severity, and implications. This information is fed back to the school community, which works through it collaboratively, seeking possible options for action. The process of a faculty working toward a common resolution is just as important–indeed in some cases possibly more important–than the active resolution itself. Action can take the form of structural changes to the way the school functions with a view to improving the way it works. Finally, a school that is working better as a developing organization can put its energies into its real purpose—teaching and learning. This kind of developing school is already a learning community.

The four phases of School Development constitute a process that is valuable to a faculty learning about itself and helping to evolve an organizational culture of collaboration and mutual accountability. It is also time-consuming and, by definition, can involve the entire faculty—and very often the wider community—in data gathering, experimentation, and discussion. The beginning of the School Development process requires a considerable investment of time from administrators encouraging school-wide involvement. As the faculty becomes more committed to working as a community and as it gains more experience in working collaboratively the emphasis can shift from school-wide issues to classroom practice.

Quality Learning Circles are mechanisms for continuing the momentum established by a school-wide School Development initiative and carrying that momentum through to the classroom. The purpose of the Quality Learning Circles is to encourage teachers to reflect on what it is they are doing in their classroom practice and to develop new understandings about teaching and learning. Many of the assumptions and processes that are used in large group School Development activities are just as appropriate at the classroom level, but the scale is smaller and much more finely textured. Whereas the goal of School Development is generally some form of group consensus, Quality Learning Circles encourage and support the meeting of student learning needs through a focused exploration with colleagues of more appropriate approaches to instructional practice. They provide one way for teachers to see each other at work and then to reflect on what they observe their colleagues do and what they do themselves. Quality Learning

Circles are concerned with professional development through a sequence of themes that forms a natural progression throughout the school year. This process is called Thematic Supervision to distinguish it from more problem-centered approaches to classroom supervision, such as "in-class" or "clinical" supervision. Thematic Supervision shares with the latter approaches an emphasis on encouraging formative and supportive feedback among members of the faculty. With the Quality Learning Circles, it is limited to issues of classroom practice, curriculum, and student growth and development. The arrangements for Quality Learning Circles and Thematic Supervision are not designed to address school-wide or policy issues. They should seek only to complement and support a continuing School Development process.

School Development, Quality Learning Circles, and Thematic Supervision are developmental processes intended to support school communities and teachers in becoming more effective in what they are attempting to achieve. They are designed to help schools, principals, and teachers be more reflective about what they do and why they do it. Through collaboration and reflection the individuals who make up the school organization learn and grow from their interaction with each other and build on their collective strengths. Since this individual growth is reflected in the way that the school becomes more effective as an organization, the school itself grows stronger in its purpose. There is a note of caution, nonetheless. An important feature of these processes that contributes to their effectiveness also serves to limit their scope. School Development, Quality Learning Circles, and Thematic Supervision are developmental processes rather than appraisal tools. Administrators who attempt to use these processes strictly to appraise the performance of teachers will quickly find resistance. The techniques work because they are nonthreatening and teachers are not at risk in sharing their professional practice with colleagues.

Still, teacher appraisal is an important challenge for administrators. With the increasing calls for accountability it has become more public and demanding. There are two approaches for meeting this challenge. As described in Part IV, principals need to have some way of appraising the performance of teachers on a consistent, regular basis, and boards of education, through district superintendents, require a similar process for appraising the performance of principals and schools. The job description is at the heart of appraisal. Principals and teachers should be appraised on their performance against a clear statement of performance expectations. These expectations should begin with a Conceptual Job Description and be elaborated through a process of regular appraisal meetings with each member of the faculty. The framework for appraisal is a cycle of regular consultations between those undertaking the appraisal and those being appraised. As part of teacher appraisal, a Professional Development Consultation cycle enables teachers to meet with the appraising administrator at least three times during the school year to formally establish, monitor, and report on the achievement of professional and personal objectives related to classroom teaching and learning.

In the next chapter all of these approaches are brought together in the School Development Spiral. This is a construct that again suggests the cyclic nature of school and individual development, but adds the dimension of a continual outward spiral of growth; of the school developing as a learning organization.

The case study selected to illustrate the spiral in Chapter 10 is Eastown Elementary School. Eastown adapted the School Development process to its own particular circumstances. Nonetheless all the components of the process are there. Schools cannot slavishly accept a change process imposed from outside, but must adapt new understandings about change to their own circumstances. Eastown had the advantage of a skillful, insightful principal who quickly understood throughout the school's own process of school development that she too, like Eastown students, teachers, and parents, was as much a learner in the process as they were.

Chapter 10

The School
Development Spiral

A school's first time through the four-phase cycle lays the groundwork for all subsequent school development activities. It is likely that considerable time will be taken progressing through the initial three stages in the first instance. This is a period of important teacher development and is the foundation for all future work. Not only are the procedures and strategies of school development being tested for their usefulness, but also a different set of norms for relating to each other is most likely being introduced to the faculty. For example, many will appreciate for perhaps the first time that it is not always necessary, or even desirable, for everyone at the school to adhere to an identical set of aims. What is necessary is that everyone knows precisely what is valued by individuals and the group and has well-established protocols for agreeing to travel in a particular direction together for a time.

During this period, faculties will come to appreciate and accept the following features of the school development process:

- There are opportunities for discussion about educational philosophies and teaching approaches that teachers within the organiza-

A school's first time through the four-phase cycle lays the groundwork for all subsequent school development activities.

tion may follow. The open acceptance of differing starting points should be encouraged.

- The expression of differences will be seen as essential to the operation of the school. Every member of the organization should have the chance to influence the direction and mode of operation of the school. Dialogue should be encouraged between those representing the administration and classroom teachers, between the many groups within the school, and between the school and its community.

- Conflict is endemic in most organizations and should be expected to be so in schools. By acknowledging its existence and dealing with it openly school effectiveness will be increased.

- School development acknowledges that teachers are sometimes resistant to change. By continually exploring options for change, reasons for their resistance can be discussed openly and the energy previously committed to blunting initiatives, rather than being increased, can be redirected.

- A school development process cannot be imposed from without, although outside support can often be helpful.

- The process assumes that a thorough knowledge of the organizational processes in a school is a necessary prerequisite to intelligent change.

- School development involves the participants in gathering their own data. This ensures a high commitment to any implications suggested by the data. A school is ready to benefit from a school development strategy if the faculty can demonstrate that variety and disagreement are valued and that working collaboratively is a preferred mode.

The aim of the first cycle of phases is to develop a culture of collaboration and to establish a pattern of collective problem solving with which faculty members can become familiar. Once established, this four-phase cycle provides a blue-print for future collaborative action. Each initiative for school development can be approached using the same sequence: first, a period of data gathering and reflection; second, collaborative problem solving; third, the consequential structural changes; and finally, the focusing on programs, curricula, and student outcomes. In this way the four-phase sequence comes to look more like a spiral as the process spreads outward, with new initiatives that begin the next round of data collecting (see Figure 10.1).

There are many issues, real or perceived, that can become the school's focus for school development. The following case study of East-own Elementary School illustrates these phases of development in action. Eastown's issues are common to many schools.

The four-phase sequence comes to look more like a spiral as the process spreads outward.

Eastown Elementary School: The Case for Change

Eastown is one of those schools on the margin between the urban city district and sprawling suburbs. Over the years the character of the school and its community has changed. When it was built in the 1970s, Eastown Elementary was a school on the outer fringes of a suburb that had a predominantly white, middle-class parent community. Over the years, as the suburban sprawl first enveloped then spread beyond Eastown, both the community and the school changed. Eastown became typical of many schools at a city's margin, with an almost equal mix of students from white, African-American, and recent immigrant Hispanic homes. Also quite typically, these more recent members of the parent community had little to do with the school, and student progress was often a reflection of this attitude. Teachers at Eastown were dutiful and caring, yet worked in the isolation of their own classrooms or grade level groups. It was expected that teachers would cover the district curriculum, and the principal saw to this expectation through a practice of periodic supervisory visits and brief discussions of the teacher's revealed shortcomings. The teachers' development took the form of attendance at occasional inservice workshops according to the interest and inclination of the teachers themselves or suggestions from the principal.

One such workshop on literacy development was attended by a group of five Eastown teachers and the Eastown principal, Anne. Its message struck a chord. Eastown had previously been informed by the district administration that schools were to review their reading resources and make bids to the district for new graded reading textbooks or other resources that would meet the requirements of the district reading curriculum. The Eastown group saw an opportunity for change.

At first Anne encouraged the enthusiasm of the small group of teachers merely by taking an interest in what they were trying in their classrooms. She did not admit it but privately knew that she had neither the understanding nor the confidence to offer supportive pedagogical advice. A few in the group had already abandoned the existing basal reader and were using trade books as their reading resource. Others, particularly two teachers from the middle and upper grades, were beginning to make links between reading and writing, abandoning the existing schedule slots and seeking a longer block of time. Yet, things were not working out. The key issue for each teacher was the number of disruptions that occurred whenever they tried to expand their classroom schedule to accommodate changes they were making in their instructional practice. It was obvious that the implications went beyond a single classroom. A meeting was convened with the principal. It was agreed that the group was to come to the faculty with their ideas as to how a longer language arts block might be established in the school schedule. In its own way Eastown had begun a process of school development.

The First Spiral Loop: The Beginning of School Development

Phase 1. Data Gathering

The Eastown weekly faculty meeting was not a professional forum, but simply the traditional way the administration could get information to the faculty. Occasionally matters were raised that could be discussed, but essentially the meeting for most teachers involved hearing information about organizational matters and the resultant gripes and grumbles that were public enough not to be left to the undercurrents and concerns usually dealt with in the parking lot. As often as Anne had attempted to change the character of the faculty meeting there was a sufficient weight of administrative matters and opinions to ensure that the closely timed hour-long meeting had a full agenda.

It was into this arena that the five teachers opened their discussion about the schedule. The teachers explained their initiative. The number and timing of students being withdrawn from their classrooms, the tradition of "snack" time, scheduled "specials" like art, music, and physical education—even the current schedule of teacher preparation time—they noted, were all impediments to establishing a longer block of time for language arts. They put a question to their colleagues: "Would the faculty be prepared to consider other scheduling options to enable this group to create longer time blocks?"

The response of the faculty was interesting. The discussion that ensued, rather than address-

The discussion that ensued brought forward issues and concerns from other members of the faculty about impediments to the things they were attempting in their own classrooms.

ing the question directly, brought forward issues and concerns from other members of the faculty about impediments to the things *they* were attempting in their own classrooms. One issue was the purpose of the faculty meeting itself and how unhelpful it proved in addressing professional issues. Another was the disruptive way that the public address system was being used to broadcast messages of little consequence to the majority of the staff. The 30 minutes given to the original issue evaporated. From the discussion two clear themes emerged. The first concerned the use of time, and the second concerned the effectiveness of the school's communication networks. The principal proposed that the faculty as a whole take the first issue as the topic for the next faculty meeting. She requested each member to consider two questions: "What do I value in our current scheduling arrangements?" and "What would I like to see changed?" Anne was recognizing that the first step in getting the faculty to work together was the need for data gathering.

Phase 2. Collaborative Analysis

This was not a faculty that had worked collaboratively on issues, yet at the subsequent faculty meeting teachers worked well enough together in their mixed groups to discuss their responses. As the groups reported their findings, Anne was aware that at least two positions were emerging. There were those who were firmly defending the status quo, and there was a large group of others who saw real advantage in reconsidering the basis on which scheduling decisions were made. Another question was posed. It concerned the amount of time that Eastown students were actively engaged in learning activities during the school day. The question arose from a group of third-grade teachers surveying their own schedules and describing a typical student's day in the classroom. They had discovered that much student learning time during the school day was being lost through movement to and from the classroom, traditional breaks in the program such as snack, periods before and after recess, and the withdrawing of students for special programs. These were similar issues to those raised by the five teachers who sought a longer time block in the first place. The data were disturbing enough to bring the faculty discussion back to the original question about creating longer opportunities for teachers to take a greater responsibility for their own students, particularly in language arts.

Phase 3. Structural Change

Anne was beginning to see a real opportunity to support her five teachers, and hopefully more. She now had a clearer focus for the scheduling issue. How could there be an improvement in the amount and quality of the time spent on learning by the students at Eastown? Anne was also beginning to experience a sense of mild frustration, but she was learning, as she put it, "that the time taken in getting people on the train, and not just to the station, is time well spent preparing for the journey." Too often, she said, there are those still on the platform when the train has gone. There were also those on the faculty who saw no value in change. Their resistance had hardened. For the most part they were specialist teachers who could see their own jobs threatened by any change that took from their care students referred for special attention. They were not the only resistors. There were also teachers who liked clearly delineated subject matter and instruction confined to shorter teaching periods. At this stage at least, they had to be supported.

Over the next two faculty meetings, working

The time taken in getting people on the train, and not just to the station, is time well spent preparing for the journey.

mainly but not exclusively in groups, the faculty considered all their options for improving the time spent on learning by students. They had continually gathered more data about specialist periods, the impact of recess on the continuity of instruction and the duty schedule of teachers, the learning progress of students withdrawn from the classroom, and other information that was relevant. It was apparent even to the least enthusiastic that some changes were both desirable and inevitable. After considerable debate, the following was agreed:

- Snack time would be quietly abandoned as a classroom tradition. It was found, for example, that some students snacked within 45 minutes of their lunch time;
- Recess would become voluntary, with the caveat that students had an appropriate break during the morning as the teacher saw fit. Teachers would be responsible for supervising their own students at break;
- Specialist periods would be completely rescheduled so that each class could schedule as many mornings or afternoons as possible without a specialist period. This would prove to be complex, but not altogether impossible. It was found that the existing arrangements were somewhat arbitrary and heavily weighted toward organizational, not learning, priorities.

Phase 4. A Focus on Teaching and Learning

The result was generally accepted. For those who sought the longer block of time for language arts there was great enthusiasm for the proposed structural changes. For those who had actively or passively rejected the new concept there was relief that their existing pattern of work would not be subject to profound and unwanted change. Even under the proposal, life for some could go on as it had before. For those who remained for the time in the middle–those who had participated but were not yet committed–there was now room for them, when they were ready, to make changes to their classroom practice without the previously existing level of structural impediments.

These small structural changes had a significant impact in two important ways. First, teachers could now focus on the real business of the school: teaching and learning. Second, and probably more important at this stage from a school development point of view, Eastown now had a process in place for dealing with issues that faced it as a school community. Anne could also gain some satisfaction from the fact that she had succeeded in bringing almost her entire faculty along with the change. There was still work to be done, and of course, every question that appeared to have an answer immediately raised many more.

The Second Loop: Communication

The second of the two issues raised at the faculty meeting that initiated the change process concerned communication. Anne had inherited with her principalship three traditional ways to disseminate information at Eastown: the weekly faculty meeting; personal memoranda; and the public address system to classrooms and areas throughout the school. Regarding the public address system, if somebody–student, faculty member, or staff –had to be informed about something, however important or trivial, a member of the office staff made a school-wide announcement, disturbing the entire school. Also, anyone in areas bypassed by the system missed the message. The flow of information by all three means was generally one way–from the administration

Eastown now had a process in place for dealing with issues that faced it as a school community.

to the faculty and staff. Communication had not been an issue before it was raised at the faculty meeting, but more than ever it was becoming one. The change in the form and content of the faculty meeting through the rescheduling process had meant that faculty administrative matters were being dealt with by more loudspeaker messages and heavier memoranda. The problem was growing and Anne knew it.

Phase 1. Data Gathering

Anne now had a forum for the faculty to deal with the communication issue. This time she went about the process in a more ordered and deliberate way, extending the issue to include communicating with parents. Anne had quietly let be known her own views about how she felt communication could be improved. Nonetheless, she asked for data through a series of questions to faculty, staff, and parents:

- How do you currently find out what is going on in the school?
- What is the most effective way information gets to you now?
- Do you feel you can respond to the information you receive?
- How would you respond to that information?
- How can we as a school improve our communication networks?

Phase 2. Increasing Collaboration

With agreement from the faculty a group of parents was invited for part of the next faculty meeting. Before their arrival the school-wide communication issue was addressed. Anne was surprised and pleased at the speed and commitment the faculty brought to the task, and happily, how some of her own suggestions had surfaced. It was clear from the discussion of the communication issue that there existed confusion about which issues were really important to the life and work of the school. Some form of managing communication and deciding priorities was required.

Phase 3. Structural Change

The structural changes proposed came quickly and without too much debate. It was agreed that:

- a Friday newsletter would be prepared for the faculty and staff, setting out special arrangements for the following week and items that the members of the school needed to know;
- a daily update would be appended to attendance sheets. In return for this service and the Friday newsletter, all faculty and staff committed themselves to read the material and respond promptly when requested;
- the public address system would be restricted to urgent messages during the day that could not be communicated in any other way, and to similar messages from the principal following the pledge, before the first lunch sitting, or before afternoon dismissal, but only if necessary.

The changes were put into effect immediately, and for the first three weeks worked well. On one occasion Anne was reminded by a teacher about the length of a message before dismissal, and she had to chase up responses to requests in the newsletter from three or four teachers. She was quick to remind them in turn that the commitment to a prompt response was their collective idea as a trade-off for fewer classroom disruptions.

Eastown had cleared some of the debris from past practices by abandoning old and inadequate structural concepts for changes that offered teachers a chance to sharpen their focus on teaching and learning.

Parent communication was more problematic. Only two parents attended the faculty meeting, both active members of the PTO. Could a faculty meeting be too intimidating for some parents? Anne would give the issue more thought. In the meantime suggestions for informal open occasions for groups of parents to visit classrooms and a revamped parent newsletter would be worked on by the PTO parents and two members of the faculty.

Phase 4. Focus on Teaching and Learning

There was much more work to be done with parent communication. Yet, Eastown had cleared some of the debris from past practices by abandoning old and inadequate structural concepts for changes that offered teachers a chance to sharpen their focus on teaching and learning. The question now was how they used the time made available by opportunities for a longer language arts block and a less disruptive instructional environment.

The Third Spiral Loop: Teacher Development

Throughout this book a distinction has been made between *school* and *individual* development. This has been done, not because development of the school and the individuals who comprise it are mutually exclusive, but because in a complex organization such as a school, the conceptual separation of the organization and the individual allows them to be broken down into more manageable components. When dealing with aspects of individual development, we are at the same time talking about another way that organizations grow and develop.

Phase 1. Data Gathering

As far as the individual development of teachers at Eastown was concerned, Anne was aware that neither she nor the teachers who had taken the initiative in the teaching and learning of reading and writing had a sufficient understanding of these processes to take their own development much further. After discussing this issue with an interested group of teachers (the number had increased to eight members of the faculty) Anne considered using an outside consultant to initiate a program of literacy development. It was agreed that the matter should be put to the faculty.

Phase 2. Collaborative Analysis

Among the faculty was a mix of uncertainty, disagreement, and support. In the end the faculty agreed to a year's trial of The Learning Network, a teacher development initiative with a literacy focus (see Appendix B). There was to be a review of progress after the trial period.

Phase 3. Structural Change

During the year an outside consultant from The Learning Network, referred to as a "program coordinator," worked with two of the teachers to develop them as "teacher leaders." The two teachers were to be a resource available to support and guide other teachers on the faculty in subsequent years. During that first year the teacher leaders put in place new practices in the teaching and learning of literacy in their own classrooms based on their developing understandings of the reading and writing processes.

The review of the first year of this initiative was mostly positive and supportive. There was

Through this cycle of action plans, observation, and instructional dialogue, Anne not only recognized the power of the reflective process, but began to recognize her own personal and professional growth.

some discussion about the cost of the consultant for the work with teacher leaders and how that expenditure could be to the detriment of other faculty wishing to attend more traditional inservice programs. There was also a question about teachers who had expressed a wish not to work with the teacher leaders. Two teachers who were unsupportive of the initiative had transferred out of the school without losing either face or dignity. Anne saw this option as compatible with the new direction the school was taking. It was important, she stressed with the faculty, that teachers feel personally comfortable with this direction. The faculty supported a second year of consultative support.

Phase 4. Focus on Classroom Practice

In this second school year, with the continued support of the consultant, each of the two teacher leaders worked part-time with six teachers, supporting those teachers' development of understanding and practice in their own classrooms. Each teacher developed an action plan, which was a specific step the teacher wanted to take in his or her own understandings and classroom practice. The teacher leader and principal would then observe a classroom episode based on the teacher's action plan. This was Eastown's form of Thematic Supervision. The themes were individualized and arose from what the teacher was doing in the classroom. Following the observation, the teacher leader used the steps of the reflective process to support the teacher toward the development of new understandings about classroom practice and to consider a new action plan leading to his or her next learning step. The principal was present throughout this process, observing both the teacher leader and the teacher engaging in the reflective process. Through this cycle of action plans, observation, and instructional dialogue, Anne not only recognized the power of the reflective process, but began to recognize her own personal and professional growth. In total, the school worked through the process for four years before every teacher who had been on the faculty when the initiative had begun had the benefit of a teacher leader's support.

There were other significant aspects of teacher development that emerged in Eastown in less formal ways. Teachers were encouraged to leave their classroom doors open (in many districts there are legal constraints against this possibility). Not all teachers did, and the option was probably more symbolic than purposeful, but it served the new willingness of the faculty to have parents, other teachers, and the administration welcomed into the classroom throughout the day. Teachers remarked how students had settled quickly into an expectation that classrooms were more accessible environments, and that visitors might be expected at any time. As it evolved the open-door policy meant ideas, achievements, and frustrations could be shared among colleagues as part of the growing mutual responsibility teachers felt for each member of the school community.

The faculty room was also becoming a focal point for professional discussion. There was less informal discussion about what students were not doing, or could not do, and much more about what they could do and how teachers might take their learning further. Overall, teacher attitudes toward their job, their colleagues, and their students were more candid and positive.

The faculty meeting had completely changed in character. It was now a professional forum. Anne and the other administrators joined the group as participants. The leaders were those whose topics had won a place on the floor. For the many visitors who were invited to participate it was a refreshing and encouraging experience. In a very real sense, Eastown had most of the pieces in place for its own continual self-renewal.

Teacher Appraisal

Development is only part of the story. Schools, principals, and teachers are also accountable to their communities. The district of which Eastown Elementary School was part required principals to conduct an appraisal of teacher performance each year. The guidelines were scant and listed only a few performance criteria. The bottom line was whether or not the teacher was performing to at least a minimal expectation. Anne sought the faculty's assistance to develop a set of Eastown criteria for teacher performance. By the time this issue was brought to the faculty, Eastown teachers were working well together as a faculty. To others they described themselves as a learning community, but the appraisal issue was a new challenge. There were sufficient sensitivities in the issue to make any approach tentative, though in the end the faculty believed it came down to a matter of teacher growth and development. They argued that teachers should be willing and able to show evidence of their growth in both their *understandings* about teaching and learning and their development in classroom *practice*. These professional attributes, they argued, should be the criteria for an appraisal. There was sufficient agreement on these broad criteria for Anne to claim consensus.

Principals in Anne's district were required to report that the teachers were performing at least to a minimum level of competence. To these reports Anne appended information about teachers' current strengths and their developmental progress through the use of their action plans and classroom observation. In the four years that she had led the school development initiative, more than fifty percent of Anne's time was spent out of her office and in classrooms. It was a significant increase over her previous pattern of activity, and a marked change in the way she perceived her role. In one sense the Professional Development Consultation cycle discussed in Chapter 9 was already in place through the work of the teacher leaders. In another sense, part of Anne's time was spent supervising that work through her own cycle of appraisal. The Professional Development Consultation was realized in Eastown by Anne's way of talking with teachers about their work and ensuring that the action plan was part of a regular expectation and a key instrument in professional development.

The Essential Features of School Development

The initiative for change in Eastown Elementary had been improvement in the teaching and learning of literacy, but this has also become the vehicle for wider change. Eastown teachers have since changed the way they teach math, how they integrate new technology as a tool for learning, and how the other subjects of the curriculum become essential topics for reading and writing. Few vestiges of the earlier Eastown remain. Even the nature of the teacher hiring policy is different, ensuring that teachers who come to work in Eastown are aware of the high expectations and commitment expected. Of course, nothing is perfect. Eastown still has its share of problems, challenges, and issues, like schools anywhere. The essential difference is that Eastown has the mechanism to deal with them. Through the processes of school and individual development, and through cycles of teacher appraisal, Eastown remains a developing school with growing strengths. Eastown is not just *becoming* a learning community–it works *as* a learning community.

As Eastown moved through the various

Through the processes of school and individual development, and through cycles of teacher appraisal, Eastown remains a developing school with growing strengths.

phases of the School Development process, the principal, teachers, and parents could recognize the ways in which the process influenced the life and work of their school. For example, when the literacy initiative began at Eastown, change became inevitable. The faculty's approach to the process of school development was a way of collaboratively managing the change process. As understandings grew and practices changed, there were also opportunities for the faculty and parents to discuss different approaches and why they were being introduced. To the Eastown community the expression of differences was essential to the development of the school. Each member of the school organization needed the opportunity to influence the direction and way development and change occurred. Dialogue was encouraged between those representing the administration and the faculty, between the groupings of opinions within the school, and between the school and its community. In this example of the school development process in action, we have not dwelt upon the sharper edges of conflict at Eastown. The potential for and reality of disagreement and how these distractions were dealt with became part of its developmental progress. By acknowledging the existence of conflict and dealing with it openly, its impact at Eastown was less disruptive to the process.

Eastown did not strictly follow the pattern of School Development set out in Part II of this book, yet most of the elements are there. For one thing, the faculty developed a thorough knowledge of the existing organizational processes as a necessary prerequisite to intelligent change decisions. It will be recalled that the Eastown faculty surprised itself when it gathered data about scheduling as a first step toward School Development. Data gathering to understand the way the school worked as an organization was an essential part of considering change options. Eastown was ready to benefit from a School Development strategy when the faculty demonstrated that with the data it had gathered, it was prepared to work collaboratively toward acceptable options for change.

A Progressive Spiral

A school such as Eastown that works through a single cycle of School Development creates its own culture of collaboration. It establishes a pattern of collective problem solving that becomes the way the school deals with issues and problems. Once established, this four-phase cycle provides the framework for future collaborative action. As each new element in the process is introduced, the same sequence of data gathering, collaborative analysis, and structural change continues to offer greater opportunities to focus on teaching and learning. The process itself becomes the way a school develops into a learning community. This cycle also expands as a spiral, broadening its impact on the school community and the way the school develops as an organization. Figure 10.1 illustrates the school development spiral of the Eastown Elementary School through which the sequence of phases that each element of development progressed during the first eight school months. Eastown is a *developing* school. Its spiral of development is the way it continues to develop as a learning community.

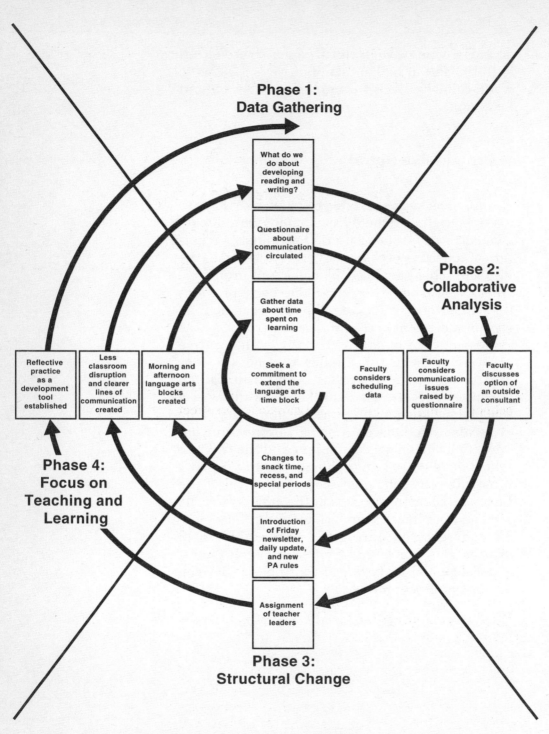

Phase 1:
Data Gathering

Phase 2:
Collaborative
Analysis

Phase 4:
Focus on
Teaching and
Learning

Phase 3:
Structural Change

What do we do about developing reading and writing?

Questionnaire about communication circulated

Gather data about time spent on learning

Seek a commitment to extend the language arts time block

Faculty considers scheduling data

Faculty considers communication issues raised by questionnaire

Faculty discusses option of an outside consultant

Reflective practice as a development tool established

Less classroom disruption and clearer lines of communication created

Morning and afternoon language arts blocks created

Changes to snack time, recess, and special periods

Introduction of Friday newsletter, daily update, and new PA rules

Assignment of teacher leaders

Figure 10.1: The Developmental Spiral Through Eight Months
at Eastown Elementary School

Chapter 11

Transactional and Transformational Leadership

Throughout this book the authors have been examining the process by which the members of a school community develop the capacity to reflect on the nature and purpose of their work together. They have been proposing models and strategies that have developed from their work with schools and with groups of principals and teachers. In Part I they found that this approach to School Development is not a unique or idiosyncratic one, and that it is consistent with a number of schools of research and thought that have been documented in international literature in recent years. In this final chapter another very topical school of management thinking that provides an even firmer foundation for a School Development approach is introduced.

In 1978 James McGregor Burns proposed a distinction between what he called *transactional* and *transformational* styles of leadership (Burns 1978). Recently a number of writers (Sergiovanni 1991; Leithwood 1992; Fullan 1992; Mitchell and Tucker 1992) have come to see this duality as

273

In a transactional culture "what gets rewarded gets done," while in a transformational culture "what is rewarding gets done" (Sergiovanni 1992, 41–45).

In a transformational culture members are committed to the mission of the organization and work to achieve those objectives.

being quite critical to an understanding of effective leadership in educational institutions.

Thomas Sergiovanni succinctly draws the distinction between the two. In a transactional culture "what gets rewarded gets done," while in a transformational culture "what is rewarding gets done" (Sergiovanni 1992, 41–45). As the name suggests, a transactional culture is based around expectations of exchange and reward. Members belong to an organization because the rewards they receive equal or exceed the investment of time and effort they are called upon to make. In such organizations leaders obtain compliance from members by offering an appropriate mix of economic, political, and/or psychological incentives. This style of leadership works best when both leaders and followers understand and agree on the key tasks to be performed. The leader's task is to keep members working on task by rewarding high performance and discouraging poor performance.

In a transformational culture members are committed to the mission of the organization and work to achieve those objectives. In this case, "what we believe in, think to be good, and feel obligated to do gets done." Transformational leadership arises when leaders are more concerned about gaining general commitment and participation from organizational members than they are about getting particular tasks done.

Schools are loosely coupled, complex organizations with unclear and often conflicting goals. This means that mere compliance with convention or policy will not be enough. It is literally not possible to specify precisely what each teacher should be doing and the standard that is expected in every activity. A transactional leader will invest much effort in developing goal statements and performance objectives, developing programs for instruction and appraisal, establishing reporting relationships, and standardizing practice. But all of this effort may have only a meager impact on classroom teaching and learning. A transformational leader will recognize that it is important to generate a shared culture within the school community and that a principal needs to direct his or her efforts to building and strengthening the shared value system of the school. Significant change at the classroom level will come about through each teacher subscribing to a new set of educational values and all teachers working collaboratively to devise teaching and learning strategies that support those values (Mitchell and Tucker 1992, 32).

In the same way as the authors have claimed a varied theoretical parentage for School Development, a number of writers have traced the scattered antecedents of transformational leadership. Mary Poplin suggests a particularly eclectic blend:

> Deci and Ryan (1985) tell us that we are motivated through a sense of competence, control, and connection. Learning theory tells us that we grow as we extend knowledge by experimenting and creating new meanings. Critical theory suggests we can advance community growth by promoting critical dialogue. Feminine theory suggests that growth happens in conjunction with others to whom we feel connected and for whom we care (1992, 11).

The common thread running through these theoretical positions is the belief that successful leadership in dynamic schools can be seen as a result of a particular form of school culture. A clear contrast exists between the culture of a school with a *transactional* style of leadership and one with a *transformational* style.

The purpose of supervision in a transactional school is to uncover weak teaching practice by direct observation and to assist teachers in improving their teaching practice.

The Transactional School

A school that exhibits a predominantly transactional culture is one where there is an unwritten contract about the way things work. The administration, for example, is seen and expected to be "in charge." Decisions about what is acceptable or expected tend to flow downward. Opinion leaders who have staked a place in the middle ground between administrators and the rest of the faculty spend much time "transacting" between the two positions. Consequently, they have greater frequency of contact with administrators and become an important group of power brokers within the school organization. This also means that ideas about change are also brokered, suggesting that unless ideas gain acceptance from the opinion makers they may proceed no further.

Supervision within a Transactional School

Supervision plays an important role within the efficient transactional school. Each teacher is expected to cover the curriculum using an appropriate repertoire of professional skills. These skills are those that are observable and capable of specification. The purpose of supervision in a transactional school is to uncover weak teaching practice by direct observation and to assist teachers in improving their teaching practice. The school administrators exercise control and influence by knowing what is going on and providing advice to overcome observed shortcomings in professional practice.

Teaching within a Transactional School

Unfortunately, this kind of hierarchical, problem-focused supervision does not work very well. Teachers come to resent the constant focus on their shortcomings and counter this perceived threat to their professional status by reducing the risks they take in their work. Instead of welcoming the supervisor's insights and assistance, they make sure that their observed instructional episode is well-rehearsed and "by the book." As well, teachers in transactional environments where supervision is perceived as part of an appraisal process are much less likely to engage in collaboration about teaching and learning. The result is a supervision process that is ineffective and possibly even counterproductive. Far from improving classroom teaching and learning, this form of supervision may confirm minimal competencies, shrink the teaching act to a set of specified task performances, and reduce student learning to a form of knowledge accumulation.

A transactional style of supervision is characterized by reluctant participants who need to be coerced to take part, and usually only do so after protective protocols and provisions are put into place. Bargaining and transacting agreements consume large portions of time that could be otherwise devoted to teaching and learning issues. Transactional supervision, as the term suggests, requires teachers to be part of the transactional process. For many, the mandated requirements for accountability upon which transactional supervision is based, by and large, lie outside the teacher's control. Teachers are not in a position to bargain about the rules for their appraisal.

The Transformational School

The transformational school is organized and described as a learning community. At the center of the learning community is a set of beliefs, values, and norms, in addition to shared understandings that constitute its core culture. Provid-

Relationships within a transformational school emphasize collaboration and interdependence.

ed that teachers subscribe to the core culture and base their work on these beliefs, values, and norms, they have considerable discretion in how they choose to teach.

Relationships within a transformational school emphasize collaboration and interdependence. Time and energy have been invested in establishing a core culture. There is greater understanding about the vision and beliefs that individuals bring to, and share within, the community of learners. There is a commitment to the core culture and the understandings that arise from it about teaching and learning. There is acceptance of the school as a community that celebrates its diversity with its variety of experiences, backgrounds, and opinions, while recognizing its common and shared mission. Teachers are not expected to be the same as one another or to use instructional methods circumscribed by supervisory requirements.

Supervision within a Transformational School

In Chapter 9 a teacher appraisal approach was described that is consistent with the values of a transformational school. Through the process of School Development, the school community commits time to defining and affirming the values of the school's core culture. Supervision provides opportunities for teachers to consider and discuss the connections between their understandings and classroom practices reflecting the school's developing core values.

Using a Conceptual Job Description, teachers set their own teaching and learning objectives. During the first Professional Development Consultation with the principal, the teacher's action plans and goals are monitored and professional developmental objectives are finalized through negotiation. These goals are then incorporated into the teacher development and school development themes for the year. In one example of a professional developmental approach, groups of teachers could form Quality Learning Circles in which an exchange of ideas and concepts is encouraged and time is set aside for reflection on professional practice.

Collegiality within a Transformational School

Classroom visits occurring as part of the Quality Learning Circle process help to refine understandings and are seen as an integral part of the school culture. The visitor to a colleague's classroom is the *learner*. There is no sense of "performance," and the reciprocal nature of the visits across the Quality Learning Circle group allows themes to be followed at increasing depth. What teachers learn alongside their colleagues about the nature and variety of the teaching and learning processes in their classrooms is significant and an important aspect of the operation of the school. As they spend time with each Quality Learning Circle through the year, principals also develop more detailed knowledge about what happens in classrooms.

In summary, supervision in a transformational school has a different function than it does in a transactional school. In the transformational school, supervision:

- supports the development of new understandings about teaching and learning, and through this new understanding, encourages new approaches to classroom practice;
- encourages the sharing of understandings and practices;
- offers a forum for the exchange of ideas;
- gives teachers the chance to learn from the principal when he or she is participating with them.

The essence of School Development is its emphasis on a shared culture of collaboration, community, and learning, not the methodology used to foster that culture.

Transformational Leadership and School Development

There is a real sense in which School Development can be thought of as the technology of the transformational school. The authors have suggested a process for the members of a school community to reflect on the nature and purpose of their work together; they have proposed a way of encouraging teachers to reflect on their professional practice in an active and collaborative way; they have introduced an approach for defining principals' and teachers' jobs, challenging them to look closely at the ideas and values they bring to their work and to their performance as leaders and classroom practitioners; and they have discussed systems of performance appraisals that require both principal and teachers to discuss their success in achieving the school's mission of meeting the learning needs of all its learners–students, teachers, administrators, and parents.

However, School Development is not simply a technology. While much of the discussion has been given over to processes and systems, the purpose of these processes is to support a school in establishing a collaborative learning community. The essence of School Development is its emphasis on a shared culture of collaboration, community, and learning, not the methodology used to foster that culture. The concept of transformational leadership makes this emphasis clear. A transformational style of leadership totally redefines the concept of leadership. As Edgar Schein (1985, 171) claims, "The only thing of real importance that leaders do is to create and manage culture." Transformational leadership is a way of thinking. It cannot be produced through effort, legal mandate, or formal policies. Transformational leaders "are more concerned about gaining overall cooperation and energetic participation from organization members than they are in getting particular tasks performed" (Mitchell and Tucker 1992, 32).

Leaders and members of transformational schools initially spend time and energy in establishing the core culture of the school and then continue to set aside time for defining and redefining the goals that community members wish to meet. These activities—establishing the core culture and interpreting that culture in terms of goals—are of fundamental importance and will generally take priority over simply implementing existing programs.

Conclusion

The authors have maintained throughout this book that learning is about the construction of new meaning rather than the accumulation of knowledge for its own sake. Transformational leadership encourages teachers to help their students construct meaning and knowledge that is relevant to their situation and upon which they can construct further knowledge. It also encourages teachers to work together to construct new meaning about their own work and about how the school works best. Most important, School Development is about how the members of the learning community can share their insights and understandings to the benefit of all. Transformational leadership is about fashioning a core culture that bonds the learning community together, ensuring that commitment and energy are focused on achieving the best possible learning environments for all its members. Such a community is likely to be diverse, committed, enthusiastic, and open to new and exciting ideas. Conflict will be used creatively to establish new paths to investigate. Control is exercised, not through supervision and standardization, but through a commitment to relate all activities to the core culture of the institution. Data gathering and collaboration are the practical expression of this commitment. Both activities precede any decision to make structural changes to the way the organization works. More important than all these is the purpose of initiating a process of School Development in the first place: to improve the quality of teaching and learning in schools.

Appendix A

Skills for Increasing Collaboration

As discussed in Chapter 4, the desire to increase the quantity and quality of collaborative work in a school is a good beginning for the School Development process. However, school faculties, like groups everywhere, are pluralistic in nature. They are composed of people who hold a variety of expectations about themselves and their colleagues, exhibit a wide range of attitudes and values, and have undeclared perceptions of relative role status, often based on incomplete data. In most situations it will be necessary to increase the level of interactive skills that teachers and administrators use when working with each other. The following processes may be useful when beginning to deal with these differences, to develop interpersonal relationships, and to resolve conflicts.

Although the model exercises presented here are divided into categories, in reality, skills and procedures will often cross the boundaries. The various interpersonal and intergroup skills are presented here to serve as a checklist that faculties can use to review their relationships and as a guide toward improving these relationships.

Roles, Expectations, and Appropriate Behaviors

In any faculty or group, there is usually a variety of perceptions about the roles and expectations of the faculty within the school, and of appropriate and inappropriate behaviors concerning interactions. If faculty collaboration is to be increased, it is important that norms are developed that recognize individual perceptions and needs, including those of new faculty members and existing faculty, and give a framework for future efforts. These discussions do not always have to be held in a whole-faculty setting, but it is important that the entire faculty understand that school policies and procedures are always open to discussion and possible change.

Role Clarification

The following six steps of this exercise can be used to clarify the perceptions that members of a group have of their roles and their expectations for their colleagues:

1. The exercise begins with members making notes about their own jobs in terms of what they understand they are meant to do, what they in fact do, and perhaps what they would be prepared to do in the future.

2. One member of the group who wants to clarify his or her role volunteers to serve as the focus of group attention.

3. Other members of the group make notes about their expectations of the volunteer's role—what they think he or she is responsible for and how they think he or she should do it.

4. The volunteer then states what he or she thinks others' expectations of his or her role are, and these are listed on a blackboard or chart paper.

5. The volunteer talks about his or her own conception of the role, and these points are also recorded.

6. The group discusses and renegotiates their expectations of the volunteer.

This is a fairly flexible exercise and capable of almost infinite variation. At the most basic level, members could simply discuss the notes they have made about their own roles as described in Step 1. Or, given a great deal of time, the group could work through all of the steps with each member (adapted from Pfeiffer and Jones 1975, 136).

Psychological Contracts

The entire faculty will complete the following questionnaire (adapted from Handy 1976, 51):

1. What do you expect from your school this year?

2. What do you consider the school will expect from you? List as many factors as you can.

3. Rank order your answers to the first two questions.

Communication Patterns and Networks

Relationships among the faculty are a consequence of the communication patterns and networks that exist in the organization. Much of the data gathering activity that is encouraged during Phase 1 will be concerned with the communication networks. For many years, teachers have made a point of discovering who among their students talks to whom, who leads and who follows, who takes leadership roles and who seldom speaks. A similar analysis should be undertaken among a school's faculty, including determining to what degree there exists a concern to involve the entire staff in the affairs of the school. This could be thought of as mapping the existing collaboration and examining the potential for further collaboration.

The Fishbowl or Triple Group exercise is a well-known technique for alerting faculty to these networks and potential concerns (Gorman 1974, 105).

The Fishbowl Exercise

The faculty is divided into three groups:

- Group A members are seated in a circle and given the task of holding a discussion.
- Group B members are seated in a concentric circle behind Group A and are given a particular individual in Group A to observe.
- Group C members are seated randomly around the room and have the task of viewing and listening to the total interactions.

Gorman (1974, 110–112) gives detailed illustrations of the instructions that could be given to each group. Group A is asked to try to form a cohesive group. Group B members are instructed to focus on their participant's ability to clarify the contributions from others and formulate goals, as well as to observe general behavioral traits such as helpfulness, supportiveness, aggressiveness, frequency of contributions, and so on. Group C members have the task of finding patterns in the group. They will be asked to comment on emergent leaders, who speaks most and least, and who seems to produce group support and action. Following the exercise a plenary session is convened to discuss the individual findings and reactions.

Role Play Discussions

Simulations abound for observing and improving networks in groups. All that is necessary is that the interacting group is given a situation that gets the members talking. In addition, particular behaviors, such as impatience, the insistence that everyone is heard, support for individuals rather than contributions, leadership takeover bids, and so on, must be emphasized by particular group members throughout. Observers are asked to focus on networks and patterns of behavior and, as a result of subsequent discussions, faculty are alerted to these behaviors in their work with each other.

Effective Communication Skills

Effective communication is at the heart of all interpersonal interaction. Exploring the existing communication patterns and networks in a school may reveal some weaknesses that need to be resolved before further school development can occur. However, effective communication, while vital to school development, does not necessarily lead to more effective schools on its own. This section suggests a number of processes that, while aiming to increase the accuracy of communication, are also designed to result in more effective action.

Clarifying and Elaborating Ideas by Paraphrasing

Paraphrasing is a mode of interaction that a group can adopt while it is conducting its formal business. While this mode is in operation no one is allowed to contribute to the discussion until they have paraphrased the previous speaker's contribution to his or her satisfaction.

Paraphrasing increases the listening skills that group members apply to the task at hand. Additionally, the discussion tends to remain focused on the central issue for long periods. If a participant makes a somewhat rambling contribution, not only is this immediately obvious as someone else attempts to paraphrase, but the rambling contributor is assisted to clarify his or her contribution. As a consequence, people who regularly use paraphrasing tend to present concise and clearly thought-out points of view. In addition, as the discussion is slowed down by the necessity of restating the previous speaker's position, a great deal of emotion is extracted from the situation. As a result it is possible to debate very sensitive issues. The following example illustrates this point.

The faculty of McKay Valley School met to discuss the issue of discipline in the hallways. They agreed to use paraphrasing for the first thirty minutes of the discussion. The function of the chairperson was to ensure that the paraphrasing was done in a satisfactory manner, not to summarize or direct the discussion.

The following exchange is taken from this discussion:

Elizabeth: I am always careful to walk with my class group when we go to the hall. Furthermore, prior to leaving my room I give them a reminder of how I expect them to behave.

James: You always accompany your class to the hall and each time you remind them how to behave.

Elizabeth: Yes.

James: So do I. It's important that pupils here know what is expected of them and know that this behavior will be demanded. That's what's wrong at present. Some teachers just don't care about how their classes behave.

Marie: You, James, agree with Elizabeth and you get quite annoyed with teachers who don't supervise their classes going to the hall as you do.

James: Just yesterday as our class was partly through a language lesson...

Chairperson: I'm sorry, James. This is not the time to amplify your remarks. Do you agree that Marie's paraphrase was satisfactory or do you wish to correct her perception?

James: My apologies. The paraphrase was good. I'm just pretty hot about this issue.

Chairing a Meeting

If all chairpersons observed a few simple rules, meetings would probably be more efficient and enjoyable, and participation would most likely increase. Such rules include:

- maintaining the focus of attention on the issue being discussed;
- preventing talk from wandering;
- stopping the debate when the discussion is complete;
- surveying the participants to ascertain opinions and positions.

Surveying is a useful method for testing a consensus within a meeting. After some discussion on a relatively controversial issue, the chairperson may want to determine whether the group is ready to reach a decision. Rather than putting the question to a vote or simply assuming that a consensus has been reached, the chairperson may choose to survey the group first.

Using this process, the chairperson makes a statement that seems to sum up the group's current thinking on the matter. The chairperson then invites each member of the group to comment briefly on the statement, and to indicate whether they support it. In this way all members of the group are given the opportunity to express their opinion, and the remainder of the members of the group are able to get an accurate impression of the emerging consensus. Following the survey, the chairperson is in an excellent position to decide whether to continue the discussion or to put the matter to a decision.

Decision Making and Problem Solving

Alvin Zander (1982, 14) points to the distinction between problem solving, when there is a need to pay attention to matters before and after a decision, and decision making, which he argues is just a single step in the problem-solving process. A greater share in both decision making and problem solving is most likely the way teachers would define increased collaboration. Thus, the question is not whether the faculty should be involved, but under what circumstances they should be involved. Clearly there are times when the teachers believe that the principal should act on his or her own initiative, but there are also times when they wish to become involved.

Delphi Method

This process can be used as an alternative to face-to-face conferences or committee meetings and is useful when a diverse group of professionals needs to arrive at some consensus on long-term objectives and developments.

- Each participant is given an opportunity to write what he or she thinks are the appropriate goals in the area under discussion.
- These are tabulated and a written report is given to each group member.
- Individuals are given a chance to restate their goals.
- A further tabulation and report are given, paying attention to similarities and differences. Those who deviate markedly are asked to give reasons for their choices.

The procedure is continued for two more rounds (Prebble and Stewart 1981, 69).

Ringi

This Japanese procedure is described by Zander (1982, 22) and involves the distribution of a written document among all faculty members with the instructions that each member may edit the document as desired. The process is complete when everyone agrees on a final version.

Conflict Negotiation

To encourage further development of a participating faculty, procedures need to be established so personal goals can be negotiated and renegotiated throughout a member's stay in the organization. The Professional Development Consultation (PDC) cycle (see Chapter 9) is one way of achieving this end.

Use of Third-Party Consultants

Here the group leader is concerned with encouraging the parties to clarify all of the issues involved in the conflict. His or her chief responsibility is to monitor the process by which the parties exchange their reactions. Normally it would be up to the parties to finally arrive at their own resolutions (Prebble and Stewart 1981, 152).

Faculty Confrontation Meeting

Developed by Richard Beckhard, this activity is particularly appropriate when the whole school is under considerable stress. The confrontation meeting is especially appropriate for a large school or tertiary institution. It provides a structured opportunity for people to express their concerns about the way the school is operating and to enable them to renegotiate the nature of their commitment (Prebble and Stewart 1981, 152).

Role Negotiation

When there is a conflict between two members of an organization over their mutual role expectations, this technique specifies that the participants write down three lists:

- the things that the other person should do more of;
- the things that the other person should do less of;
- the things that the other person does that are helpful and should not be changed.

Both members then select the issues that are negotiable and address the items one by one (Prebble and Stewart 1981, 154).

There are many sources for additional exercises to increase communication and collaboration in a school faculty.

Appendix B

The Learning Network

In Chapter 10 it was mentioned that Eastown School was part of The Learning Network. Some other schools that are mentioned as case studies are also part of this school and teacher development initiative. In most respects the school development process at Eastown School is consistent with the key developmental strands that have been woven throughout this book. The one clear difference in Learning Network schools is the use of an outside consultant or program coordinator, who together with the principal and teacher leaders on the faculty form the "critical triangle" of change leadership.

During the first of the two years of involvement of The Learning Network, a program coordinator works directly with the teacher leaders to develop a model of literacy teaching and learning in their own classrooms. This model is based on meeting the learning needs of students through the careful assessment of previous learning and an analysis of the student's next learning steps. In the second year, working alongside up to eight faculty colleagues each for half a day a week, the teacher leaders establish with these colleagues in their classrooms the new understandings and approaches about literacy teaching and learning. The teacher leaders are working with their teacher colleagues in the same way the program coordinator worked with them. They still have the support of the program coordinator, but the emphasis in the second year is on their teacher development role.

The mechanism for teacher development is the action plan. In the first year, the program coordinator, and in the second year, the teacher leader uses the action plan as the focus for a developmental learning step. The action plan provides the weekly classroom instructional episode that will be observed by both teacher leader and principal and becomes the focus for an instructional dialogue that follows the observation. The instructional dialogue, which is the opportunity for establishing the habit of reflective practice, also initiates the teacher's next action plan (Richard C. Owen Publishers 1996).

As part of The Learning Network, a principal commits to taking a full part in this development process. The principal, like the teacher leader and observed teacher, is expected to develop further his or her own understandings rather than simply be a passive visitor, or more significantly, an evaluator in the traditional sense. Nancy, the Eastown principal, exemplifies this active, committed perspective on teacher and school development.

An initiative to implement The Learning Network, as was the case at Eastown, is more likely to be part of Phase 3 of the School Development process, when the faculty has already identified a curriculum issue, gathered and collaboratively analyzed the data, and looked at the options for a commitment to action.

Bibliography

Adelman, Clem and Robin J. Alexander. 1982. *The Self-Evaluating Institution: Practices and Principles in the Management of Educational Change.* London, England: Methuen.

Allington, Richard. 1994. "The Schools We Have. The Schools We Need." *Reading Teacher,* Vol. 48, no. 1, September, pp 14–29.

Argyris, Chris and Donald Schön. 1978. *Organizational Learning: A Theory of Action Perspective.* Reading, MA: Addison-Wesley.

Averch, Harvey A., et al. 1972. *How Effective is Schooling? A Critical Review and Synthesis of Research Findings.* Santa Monica, CA: The Rand Corporation.

Bonstingl, John Jay. 1992. "The Quality Revolution in Education." *Educational Leadership,* Vol. 50, no. 3, November, pp 4–9.

Brookfield, Stephen D. 1995. *Becoming a Critically Reflective Teacher.* San Francisco, CA: Jossey-Bass.

Brookover, Wilbur B. and Larry W. Lezotte. 1977. *Changes in School Characteristics Coincident with Changes in School Achievement.* East Lansing, MI: Institute for Research on Teaching, Michigan State University.

Burns, James McGregor. 1978. *Leadership.* New York, NY: Harper and Row.

Clark, David L., L.S. Lotto, and Terry Astuto. 1984. "Effective Schools and School Improvement: A Comparative Analysis of Two Lines of Inquiry." *Educational Administration Quarterly,* Vol. 20, no. 3, pp 41–68.

Cogan, Michael. 1973. *Clinical Supervision.* Boston, MA: Houghton Mifflin Co.

Coleman, James, E.Q., et al. 1966. *Equality of Educational Opportunity,* Vol. 2. Washington, DC: US Government Printing Office.

Corbett, H.D., W.A. Fireson, and G.G. Rossman. 1987. "Resistance to Planned Change and the Sacred in School Cultures." *Educational Administration Quarterly,* Vol. 33, no. 4, pp 36–59.

Darling-Hammond, Linda and Eileen Sclan. 1992. "Policy and Supervision." In *Supervision in Transition: The 1992 ASCD Yearbook,* ed. C.D. Glickman, 7–29. Alexandria, VA: Association for Supervision and Curriculum Development.

Deci, E.L. and R.M. Ryan. 1985. *Intrinsic Motivation and Self-Determination in Human Behavior.* New York, NY: Plenum Press.

Dewey, John. 1933. *How We Think: A Restatement of the Relation of Reflective Thinking to the Educative Process.* London, England: Heath.

Duttweiler, Patricia C. 1990. "A Broader Definition of Effective Schools: Implications from Research and Practice." In *Target 2000: A Compact for Excellence in Texas's School,* eds. Thomas J. Sergiovanni and John E. Moore, pp 65–75. Austin, TX: Texas Association for Supervision and Curriculum Development.

Edmonds, Ronald. 1979. "Some Schools Work and More Can." *Social Policy,* Vol. 9, no. 2, pp 28–32.

Eisner, Elliot W. 1992. "Educational Reform and the Ecology of Schooling." *Teachers College Record,* Vol. 93, no. 4, Summer.

Freeston, Kenneth R. 1992. "Getting Started with TQM." *Educational Leadership,* Vol. 50, no. 3, November, pp 10–13.

Fullan, Michael G. 1992. "Visions That Blind." *Educational Leadership*, Vol. 49, no. 5, February, pp 19–20.

Goldhammer, Robert, R.H. Anderson, and R.J. Krajewski. 1980. *Clinical Supervision: Spe-*

cial Methods for the Supervision of Teachers, 2d ed. New York, NY: Holt, Rinehart & Winston.

Gorman, A.H. 1974. *Teachers and Learners: The Interactive Process of Education,* 2d ed. p 105; pp 110–112. Boston, MA: Allyn and Bacon.

Griffiths, M. and S. Tann. 1992. "Using Reflective Practice to Link Personal and Public Theories." *Journal of Education for Teaching*, Vol. 18, no. 1.

Grimmett, Peter P., Olaf P. Rostad, and Blake Ford. 1992. "The Transformation of Supervision." In *Supervision in Transition: The 1992 ASCD Yearbook,* ed. C.D. Glickman, pp 185–202. Alexandria, VA: Association for Supervision and Curriculum Development.

Halpin, Andrew H. 1966. *Theory and Research in Administration.* New York, NY: Macmillan.

Handy, Charles B. 1978. *Gods of Management.* London, England: Pan Books.

—. 1990. *Inside Organisations: 21 Ideas for Managers.* London, England: BBC Books.

—. 1976. *Understanding Organisations.* Harmondsworth, UK: Penguin.

Handy, Charles B. and R. Aitken. 1986. *Understanding Schools as Organisations.* Harmondsworth, UK: Penguin.

Hoy, Wayne K. and Cecil G. Miskel. 1982. *Educational Administration: Theory, Research and Practice,* 2d ed. New York, NY: Random House.

Johnson, David W., et al. 1984. *Circles of Learning: Cooperation in the Classroom.* Alexandria, VA: Association for Supervision and Curriculum Development.

Joyce, Bruce, et al. 1990. "The Self-Educating Teacher: Empowering Teachers Through Research." In *Changing School Culture Through Staff Development: The 1990 ASCD Yearbook,* ed. C.D. Glickman. Alexandria,

VA: Association for Supervision and Curriculum Development.

Kraus, William A. 1980. *Collaboration in Organizations: Alternatives to Hierarchy.* New York, NY: Human Sciences Press.

Leithwood, Kenneth A. 1992. "The Move Toward Transformational Leadership." *Educational Leadership*, Vol. 49, no. 5, February, pp 8–12.

Leithwood, Kenneth A. and D.J. Montgomery. 1982. "The Role of the Elementary School Principal in Program Improvement." *Review of Educational Research,* Vol. 52, no. 3, Fall, pp 309–339.

Likert, Rensis. 1967. *The Human Organization: Its Management and Value.* New York, NY: McGraw-Hill.

Little, Judith Warren. 1982. "Norms of Collegiality and Experimentation: Workplace Conditions of School Success." *American Educational Research Journal*, Vol. 19, no. 3, pp 325–340.

—. 1983. "Teachers as Colleagues." In *Educators Handbook: A Research Perspective,* ed. V.R. Koehler. White Plains, NY: Longman.

Lortie, Dan C. 1975. *School Teacher: A Sociological Study.* Chicago, IL: University of Chicago Press.

MacKenzie, D. 1983. "Research for School Improvement: An Appraisal of Some Recent Trends." *Educational Researcher,* Vol. 12, no. 4.

Macpherson, R.J.S. 1984. "A Hitch-hiker's Guide to the Universe of Tom Greenfield." *The Australian Administrator.* Deakin University, Vol. 5, no. 2.

Mitchell, Douglas E. and Sharon Tucker. 1992. "Leadership as a Way of Thinking." *Educational Leadership*, Vol. 49, no. 5, February, pp 30–35.

New Zealand Council for Educational Research (NZCER). 1990. "School Level Environment Questionnaire." Item 4, Set Number 2.

Nolan, James and Pam Francis. 1992. "Changing Perspectives in Curriculum and Instruction." In *Supervision in Transition: The 1992 ASCD Yearbook,* ed. C.D. Glickman, pp 44–60. Alexandria, VA: Association for Supervision and Curriculum Development.

Parlett, Malcolm and David Hamilton. 1977. "Evaluation as Illumination: A New Approach to the Study of Innovatory Programmes." In *Beyond the Numbers Game: A Reader in Educational Innovation,* ed. David Hamilton. London, England: Macmillan.

Peters, Thomas J. and Robert H. Waterman. 1982. *In Search of Excellence: Lessons from America's Best-Run Companies.* New York, NY: Harper and Row.

Pfeiffer, J.W. and J.E. Jones, eds. 1975. *A Handbook of Structured Experiences for Human Relations Training,* Vol. 5. La Jolla, CA: University Associates.

Poplin, Mary S. 1992. "The Leader's New Role: Looking to the Growth of Teachers." *Educational Leadership,* Vol. 49, no. 5, February, pp 10–11.

Prebble, Tom K. 1978. "Goal Dissensus and Educational Change." *Journal of Educational Administration,* Vol. 16, no. 1, pp 7–18.

Prebble, Tom K. and David J. Stewart. 1981. *School Development: Strategies for Effective Management.* Palmerston North, New Zealand: Dunmore Press.

President's Commission on School Finance. 1972. Study. Santa Monica, CA: The Rand Corporation.

Purkey, S.C. and M.S. Smith. 1982. *Effective Schools: A Review.* Madison, WI: Wisconsin School of Education Research, University of WI.

Richard C. Owen Publishers. 1996. "Understanding The Learning Network." Katonah, NY: Richard C. Owen Publishers, Inc.

Robinson, Viviane M. 1982. "School Reviews: A New Zealand Experience." *Educational Management and Administration*, Vol. 10, pp 195–202.

Rutter, Michael, P. Maughan, Ouston J. Mortimore, and A. Smith. 1979. *Fifteen Thousand Hours: Secondary Schools and Their Effects on Children*. Cambridge, MA: Harvard University Press.

Schein, Edgar. 1985. *Organization Cultures and Leadership: A Dynamic View*. San Francisco, CA: Jossey-Bass.

Schlechty, Phillip. 1990. *Schools for the Twenty-first Century: Leadership Imperatives for Educational Reform*. San Francisco, CA: Jossey-Bass.

Schön, Donald A. 1987. *Educating the Reflective Practitioner: Toward a New Design for Teaching and Learning in the Professions*. San Francisco, CA: Jossey-Bass.

—.1983. *The Reflective Practitioner: How Professionals Think in Action*. New York, NY: Basic Books.

Selznick, Philip. 1957. *Leadership in Administration*. New York, NY: Harper and Row.

Sergiovanni, Thomas J. 1996. *Leadership for the Schoolhouse: How is it Different? Why is it Important?* San Francisco, CA: Jossey-Bass.

—. 1991. *The Principalship: A Reflective Practice Perspective,* 2d ed. Boston, MA: Allyn and Bacon.

—. 1992. "Why We Should Seek Substitutes for Leadership." *Educational Leadership,* Vol. 49, no. 5, February, pp 41–45.

Sergiovanni, Thomas J. and John E. Corbally. 1984. *Leadership and Organizational Culture: New Perspectives on Administrative Theory and Practice*. Urbana, IL: University of Illinois Press.

Smyth, John. 1988. "Deliberating on Reflection in Action as a Critical Form of Professional Education." *Studies in Continuing Education*, Vol. 10, no. 2.

—. 1989. "Developing and Sustaining Critical Reflection in Teacher Education." *Journal of Teacher Education*, Vol. 40, no. 2, March/April.

Sparkes, Andrew. 1991. "The Culture of Teaching, Critical Reflection and Change: Possibilities and Problems." *Educational Management and Administration,* Vol. 19, no. 1, p 9.

Stewart, David J. and Tom K. Prebble. 1985. *Making it Happen: A School Development Process.* Palmerston North, New Zealand: Dunmore Press.

—. 1993. *The Reflective Principal: School Development within a Learning Community.* Palmerston North, New Zealand: ERDC Press, Massey University.

Tannenbaum, Arthur. 1986. *Control in Organizations.* New York, NY: McGraw-Hill.

Tannebaum, Arthur and R.A. Cooke. 1979. "Organisational Control: A Review of Studies Employing Control Graph Methods." In *Organisations Alike and Unlike,* eds. D.J. Hickson and C.J. Lammers. London, England: Routledge and Kegan Paul.

U.S. Government. 1991. *America 2000.* April 18, 1991. U.S. Government Printing Office: 1991- 298-479/40655. ED/OS91-13.

Walton, Mary. 1986. *The Deming Management Method.* New York, NY: Perigee.

Weick, Karl E. 1976. "Educational Organizations as Loosely Coupled Systems." *Administrative Science Quarterly,* Vol. 21, no. 2, pp 1–19.

—. 1986. "The Concept of Loose Coupling: An Assessment." *Organizational Theory Dialogue,* December.

Zander, Alvin. 1982. *Making Groups Effective.* San Francisco, CA: Jossey-Bass.

Index

Accountability, 90–91
Achievement, influenced by
    socioeconomic background, 33–34
Action plan, 37
Adelman, Clem, 104
Administration
  educational, 7
  standards, 217–225
Alexander, Robin, 104
Appraisal
  principal, 10–11, 197–225, 248
  systems, 22–25
  teacher, 10–11, 227–244, 248,
    268–269
Argyris, Chris, 82
Assessment, evaluation, and appraisal
  of students, 137–138
Astuto, Terry, 37

Bonstingl, John Jay, 43–45
Brookfield, Stephen, 72
Brookover, Wilbur B., 35
Burns, James McGregor, 273–274

Clark, David L., 37
Clinton, President, 19
Classroom
  culture, 189–190, 229, 232
  routines, 188–189
  teaching, 228–229, 231
Cogan, Michael, 178
Coleman, James, 33
Collaborative analysis and problem
  solving, 76–77, 86–91, 118–122,
  258–259
Collective action processes, 84, 91–92
Collegial supervision, 28–33
Commitment
  cultural, 8

of school, 37, 147–149
Common school model, 15
Communication, 83–84
  principal's responsibility for school
    communication networks, 204–205
  in school development process,
    261–264
Community relations, 145–147, 202–203
Consultant, in data collection, 107–108
Corbally, John, 41
Croft, Donald, 111
Culture
  classroom, 189–190, 229, 230, 232
  of collaboration, 8
  of commitment, 8
  managing and developing, 203–204
  perspective of school management,
    39–42
  principal's contribution, 9, 56–57
  of the school, 42, 111–113, 234
Curriculum development, 14, 29, 80–81
Curriculum and instructional program,
  190–191

Data gathering, 76–78, 81–83, 97–118
  case studies, 113–118
  overview, 100–101
  at the school level, 102–113
  on specific issues within the school,
    113–118
Deming method, 39–45
Deming, W. Edward, 39–40
Developmental process, vi, 247–272
Dewey, John, 161
Duncan, Peter, v, 10
Duttweiler, Patricia, 38–39

Edmonds, Ronald, 34–35, 39
Effective schools movement, 33–39

301